LIBRARIANSHIP IN INDIAN NATIONAL PERSPECTIVE

LIBRARIANSHIP IN INDIAN NATIONAL PERSPECTIVE

By

Subhas C. Biswas

GYAN

ISBN: 978-81-212-1279-3

Price: ₹ 475

First Published, 2015

Published by :

Gyan Publishing House
23, Main Ansari Road,
Daryaganj, Delhi-110002
Phone : 23282060, 23261060
E-mail: books@gyanbooks.com

Laser Typesetting : Shubham Printers, Delhi
Printed at : G. Print Process, Delhi

Cataloging in Publication Data—DK
Courtesy: D.K. Agencies (P) Ltd. <docinfo@dkagencies.com>

Biswas, Subhas C. (Subhas Chandra), 1932- **author.**
Librarianship in Indian national perspective / by Subhas C Biswas.
pages cm
Includes bibliographical references.
ISBN 9788121212793

1. National Library (India). 2. Library administration—India. 3. Library science—India. I. Title.

DDC 027.50954 23

For

Tutu, Kunal & Mou

Contents

Preface 9

1. National Library : In-House Action Plan for the Management 19
2. The National Library of India Must Act Fast 33
3. Indian Legal Deposit Legislation and its Impact on the National Library 47
4. Public Library Service—Users and Resources 69
5. Raja Rammohun Roy Library Foundation (RRRLF)—Future Role 83
6. Digital Library of India—The Consortium Approach 95
7. Transitional University Libraries 113
8. Library and Information Science—Academic Research 133

Index 153

Preface

A few chapters of the book are related more to the National Library of India, reflecting some of my recent thoughts. My first exposure to this library was in 1957 when I was visiting the library daily as a student trainee of a three months short term training course conducted by Bengal Library Association. Most of the teaching faculties were senior staff members of the National Library including the Librarian, B. S. Kesavan, who took special care to allow the trainees to get a first-hand exposure of the library. Secondly, he may have found it most convenient for him to allow the training course conducted at the library to avoid any kind of logistic inconvenience to his staff. In early 1940s, the collections of the Imperial Library (name changed to National Library in 1948) were temporarily housed in two separate close-by buildings (Jabakushum House and 6 Esplanade East). This was done as a safety measure from the devastating bombing of Calcutta during the second world war. The library was finally shifted to its present permanent location, the Vice-regal Palace, Belvedere followed by the enactment of the Imperial Library (Change of Name) Act of 1948. This was the time Mr Kesavan took over as the librarian of the National Library. Our classes were held in a room on the first floor of the main building where books from the famous Ashutosh Collection were preserved all along the four walls of the large room.

This library with profound grandeur of the palace building, its enchanting location surrounded by a large well maintained garden with sprawling green lawns, the beautiful collections of so many bound volumes of priceless treasure house, and impressive personality of the librarian, Mr Kesavan, and his team must have influenced me to pursue with librarianship as my future career. Whereas my previous two and a half years of working as a college librarian in a small town, got into my head the idea of being a librarian means to serve as a glorified clerk within a room full of books only. Completion of this training course helped me in getting a full-time employment at the Calcutta University Library which in turn opened the door of getting admission to the one year evening full-time Diploma Course in Library Science at the same University. I left the job and moved to London in early 1959. I was fortunate for being selected, first as a trainee at the British Museum Library, Department of Oriental Printed Books and Manuscripts, followed by a full time employment in the same Department. I served this library for over a decade. During my tenure with the Department of Culture, Government of India (1980-90), I was assigned with a job to review the acquisition policy of the National Library. The Report of the review Committee (Chairperson: Subhas C Biswas) was submitted within three months in 1983 which must be lying on some shelves of the Ministry, gathering dust. This job with the Government of India gave me an exposure to various policy issues that are directly relevant to the growth of Indian librarianship in general. This also facilitated me of visiting and meeting a large number of personalities related to library and the book world, both in and out of India. I took up several projects during this period, such as, *Bibliographic Survey of Indian Manuscripts Catalogues,* and the project on making microfilm copies of early twentieth century Indian language publications (MIPP) sponsored by the US Library of Congress and the Government of India. The latter allowed me to work closely within the administrative framework of the US Library of Congress. These two projects in particular, helped me to be familiar with a large number of different types of libraries in different parts of the country.

To include the above two paragraphs of my involvement especially with national libraries over the last several decades out of over sixty years of active librarianship, is an attempt to justify of bringing out this publication. Some of the topics have been revised for updating from the originals published in different journals over the last few years, such as, (1) *IASLIC Bulletin, (2) Granthana: Indian Journal of Library Studies, (3) Annals of Library and Information Studies and (4) Alexandria* (Manchester University Press). I am pleased to acknowledge their support and approval for allowing these to be included in the book.

A brief summary of the chapters would not be out of place, they are:

1. National Library In–House Action Plan For The Management: Over the last few decades, India's legal deposit legislation or Delivery of Books Act, 1954 did not help much the National Library to build up a comprehensive collection of Indian publications due to several shortcomings in the Act. The other two relevant Acts, Press and Book Registration Act, 1867 and Copyright Act of India, 1957 running parallel have helped in creating more confusion with the passage of time.

Central Reference Library shall not have its separate identity any longer. It shall be merged with the National Library as the Bibliographic Division; that would include full responsibility of bringing out *INB.* There are several suggestions on both long and short term action plans that are conventionally accepted as part of national library activities, such as, ISBN/ISSN identification number allocation; specialised reading areas in addition to the general reading room now in Bhasha Bhavan; underground linkages of all three main buildings; running a scholars hostel is discouraged; library's publication and research activities are to be given high priority. Exhibition, display, promotion and publicity must get high priorities and be brought under one special unit that would surely help library to be more inter-active with the patrons. Open the doors of the library to offsite users by creating a window for the 'Friends of the National Library' who would be happy to extend support to the cause of development of the library, and offer such extension activities to improve the image of the library and get out of the present stagnation and apathy.

2. The National Library of India Must Act Fast : Several issues that are having overall impact on the National Library and also directly affected its slow rate of modernisation process of Indian librarianship on the whole. Continuous downhill slide of the National Library of India over the last sixty years or so, and why it took this turn is discussed in detail. The original Calcutta Public Library which Lord Curzon converted into the Imperial library, during the colonial era and finally re-named by an Act of Parliament as the National Library (1948) continued to be following the conventional British public library operational guidelines till date. Since then several review committees (e.g., chaired by L.K. Jha, Satish Chandra, Saibal Gupta) submitted their reports but none spelled out specifically the changes required of its scope and the role in terms of services from a public library to that of a national library. To bring in the essential changes, some positive measures are to be initiated by the stakeholders immediately so as to allow it move back on the growth tracks like many other national libraries of the world. The two recently produced documents: NKC-WGL recommendations (2006) and NACONAL (2006) on Indian library services, with proposals of its future role and growth pattern are critically examined. Some significant moves taken by the management of the British Library (National Library of England) during this period to cater to the needs of users are cited here, as examples. Suggestions for some specific actions to be taken by the Government of India, National Library Advisory Board, senior management and professional organisations of librarians were presented, such as, implementing the National Library Act 1976 (with some modification), make an immediate move to fill up the sanctioned posts of senior professionals and conduct a comprehensive survey of users and their present and future requirements, revise Delivery of Books Act, 1954, merger of CRL with the National Library and take appropriate initiatives to formulate the required structure of a consortium, with required responsibilities, for setting up the National Digital Library of India. Proposed readers' survey shall help the management and policy makers to decide the future course of actions.

3. Indian Legal Deposit Legislation and its Impact on the National Library : Next we discussed the impact of India's legal deposit legislation. Over the last few decades, the Indian legal deposit legislation or Delivery of Books Act, 1954 together with the limitations in its applications has brought stagnation in every sphere of activity of the library. The act specifically stated that four regional 'public libraries' shall be the recipients (National Library for the eastern region). This obsolete concept of national library to be another 'public library' needs to be reviewed when the act is revised next. There are several countries where a library attached to a major university or central legislative assembly has being declared as the sole repository of national intellectual heritage. The other two relevant acts, Press and Registration of Books Act, 1867 and the Copy Right Act, 1957, running parallel have helped in creating more confusion within both the publishing and library world of India. Being under the direct control of the central government as a subordinate office of the Ministry of Culture has forced the library to operate within the four walls of rigid rules and regulations with very little flexibility in management and policy matters. These shortcomings have direct impact on the services of the National Library. A few suggestions are being placed on the line of action that could be considered while revising the present DB Act.

4. Public Library Service—Users and Resources : The real growth of public library movement in India has largely been activated during the post-independence period. During the seventh Five-year Plan (1985-1990), a National Policy for Library and Information Systems was formulated (1986) but this did not bring forth the public library as an equal partner with education and literacy programme to every citizenry. We brought forth the special requirements in public library management, in issues such as, manpower, active participation in all community services and to promote ICT application in day to day life. RRRLF has to shift its gears from a donor agency to support and supplement print resources of all public libraries to a more holistic approach towards allowing access to every type of information that helps to develop their intellectual abilities and other socio-cultural needs of the local community, be it entertainment, sports, art and culture or health and environment, issues relevant to their daily livelihood. With the introduction of computer and communication technologies that are having more and more direct impact on day to day life of everyone, public libraries must take a leading and proactive role in sharing its information resources and allow the users direct access to the vast non-sight information resources worldwide through internet and cloud technologies to explore other fields of human activities round the world.

5. Raja Rammohun Roy Library Foundation (RRRLF)—Future Role : It is an 'autonomous' organisation fully funded by the Central Government (Ministry of Culture) with sole objective of providing back up support to all state governments and union territories (UTs) in taking public library services to every corner of the country. For over forty years, the foundation has been active more as donor agency in providing grants to supplement the state governments mainly for collection development. Now, it is time for it to act more appropriately, as the national coordinating and monitoring agency for the overall growth and development of library and information systems and services of the country. This would also help when NML (National Mission of Libraries) transformed into a National Commission of Libraries and make the foundation to act as the main research and monitoring wing of the parent organisation. It would be logical for the foundation to adopt a more progressive policy of public library development, similar in line of changes introduced by the British government over the last several decades.

6. Digital Library of India–The Consortium Approach: Current trends in digitisation of library based, information resources in India is continued to be in fragmentary way focussing primarily on preservation of 'valuable' printed resources available in respective libraries. Besides, the speed of growth of commercial *e*-publications worldwide and similar technological innovations over the last decade raised a few questions on the very role of libraries as practiced over the previous century. Information supplied by the library and other academic support or referral services can also be made available to users direct either by the producers or in some cases, from the online databases. *Google, Amazon* and several others have joined in the race of supplying information, including digitised multimedia resources through internet access, supported by the proliferation of *e*-book reader and other text reading devices. Many higher academic and research institutions have accepted these and other social network services, like *Web 2.0* tools, to allow access to their own publications and other secondary digitised resources. It was suggested that the National Mission for Libraries may recommend for the National Library of India to take the leading role of coordinating all individual or separate institutional efforts, to constitute a national digital library that would be in a position to offer comprehensive digitised India related information to all concern. To be able of undertaking such a task the scope and operational structure of the new generation of libraries would require to be redefined.

7. Transitional University Libraries : The idea of writing on this topic came while reading an article, 'Unsustainability of The Traditional Library And The Threat To Higher Education' by Brian L. Hawkins in a book, *Mirage of continuity* edited by Hawkins and Battin, Washington DC, 1998. He presented his arguments based on his experience as the Head of Browne University Library, Rhode Islands, USA. Issues raised by him were truly relevant at that point of time in the USA and many other countries. While discussing informally with a few senior university librarians, it came to my mind that much of it is still relevant to Indian academic world. This chapter was written reflecting exclusively on current Indian university library conditions. I am deeply indebted to Brian Hawkins for encouraging me to think of Indian academic libraries in a more realist perspectives.

In today's world, libraries are claimed to be intellectual foundation of a democratic society primarily because of allowing free and open access to recorded information knowledge. But in the beginning of twenty first century, the very survival of our traditional libraries are seriously threatened. First growth of electronic media supported by similar research and development in Information and Communication Technologies (ICT) are allowing every citizenry new vistas to access information, irrespective of its source or packing format. Types of information a library traditionally provides, a substantial segment of that is now also accessible directly through internets, to a larger section of the community. This is the noticeable trends in a select number of university libraries in the western world. It is expected to be followed in more and more universities sooner than later. This trend is also being accepted as 'inevitable' in several IITs and similar postgraduate academic institutions of India. A significant factor in this domain is the direct on going involvements of *Google, Amazon* and similar such commercial portals in a very big way. A solution to this problem (not so simplistic though) for libraries is to provide electronic access to information–rather than storage of information resources. New library, especially in this sector, needs to bring together scholars and information resources without necessarily bringing either one to a physical building.

8. Library and Information Science–Academic Research: Teaching of Library and Information Science at the postgraduate level in Indian universities first started in 1937 at the University of Madras by Dr S.R. Ranganathan. The first Doctorate degree in Library Science was awarded at the University of Delhi, under his guidance, in 1957. During the last few decades, number of LIS schools increased to nearly two hundred; as a result, there has been a corresponding high increase in Ph.D. degree holders within the discipline. According to data available to us through INFLIBNET, 595 doctorate degrees were awarded by different Indian universities till 2008 in this field. Qualitative analysis of the dissertations submitted as partial fulfillment for obtaining the degree at different universities of India has never been attempted but an overall view on the trends of research by individual library professionals, other than obtaining an academic degree that was reflected through *Library and Information Science Abstracts (LISA).* It clearly indicates a significant gap in coordination for selecting research topics, either at an institutional or national level. This requires serious consideration by the professional organisations and institutions.

By being out of active librarianship for over two decades, I have to rely on some help from a large number of libraries and librarians of several institutions at various levels. At the same time, it made me perhaps, a 24×7 library professional. I owe a deep gratitude to all the staff of India International Centre Library for all their help and cooperation where I have been spending much of my time over the last few years. I am highly indebted to Dr Prakiti R. Goswami, former Director, (presently Librarian, IGNCA), Ms Charanjeet Kaur of Central Secretariat Library, Delhi for their continuous support; Dr Swapan Chakraborty, (former Director General), Ashim Mukherjee, Syed Abuzar of the National Library; Mr K.K. Kochukoshi, (former Librarian) Central Reference Library, Kolkata. RRRLF, Director (presently, Director General) Kishore Krishna Banerjee has always been kind and major source of continuous help. No words would be enough to express my sincere gratitude to Dr Narendra Kumar Chief Librarian of IIT Delhi (formerly at Delhi University, Central Library) for his response in providing required data on acquisition of Delhi University and IIT Delhi libraries within a week and to Dr Kanakben Jani, University Librarian of North

Gujarat University, Patan for her similar positive response. I sincerely feel thankful to Dr N.K. Gaur, University Librarian of Jawaharlal Nehru University, whom I am yet to meet personally, for helping me with the acquisition and expenditure figures of the university library within a week. The only exception was of Dr Soumitra Sarker, Librarian of the University of Calcutta, who could not provide me with the Central library's acquisition data even after pursuing the issue for over four months. To sum up his response, he found this job a bit too complicated and wastage of his valuable time. There are many others who helped me in so many different ways at different stages whose names are difficult now for me to put on records to express my sincere gratitude individually. However, special mention must be made of some, for their encouragement, professional support and critical comments received from Geetha Balasubramanian, B.G. Sunder Singh my former colleagues, for helping me in different ways; to Anu, Kunal and Noyona for assisting me in all types of data processing issues and extended full support to overcome various problems I faced at different times. I am greatly indebted to Dr. Jagdish Arora, Director INFLIBNET for kindly providing me with INFLIBNET database on LIS dissertations and theses accepted by Indian universities. I am grateful to Dr. Usha Kataria for her help in checking bibliographical references. I am also deeply indebted to Supratim Chatterjee, Sarmistha Bhattacharya and Manju Khanna, who were always ready to help and support me at various stages of the project. My wife Atreyi's continuous encouragement in all my professional activities needs to be recorded here separately.

Subhas C. Biswas

New Delhi, 2015

1

National Library: In-House Action Plan for the Management

Background : Lord Curzon's Imperial Library in Calcutta changed its name by an Act of Parliament to make it the National Library of India in 1948. Later it was declared an institution of national importance as per Article 62 of the Seventh Schedule of the Union List in the Constitution of India. The basic functions of the Library[1] are: (1) acquisition and conservation of all significant printed material (excluding only of ephemera) as well as manuscripts of national importance; (2) collection of print material relevant to India, irrespective of its origin; (3) rendering of bibliographic and documentary services of current and retrospective material, both general and specialised. This implies the responsibility to produce national bibliographies both currentand retrospective, on various topics of interest to India; (4) acting as referral centre, purveying full and accurate knowledge of all sources of bibliographical information and participation in international bibliographical activities; and (5) acting as a centre for international book exchange and internal loan. Above guidelines or functions were recommended by a Reviewing Committee (Jha Committee, 1969) which are still being followed broadly by the National Library.

However, for some unknown reasons the Government of India has not effectively allowed the Library to widen its scope and functions, like so many other national libraries of the world. As a matter of fact, it has not been allowed to operate effectively, other than of being a regional public library at its origin. For example, the central government only recently asked the library to specialise in eastern regional library development programme. The sectarian approach if pursued further, shall lead of not having a national library of India. On the whole, both local politics and regional parochialism have both badly affected Indian librarianship in general and the National Library in particular. The Library is administratively a subordinate office of the Ministry of Culture, Government of India. The Director General of the National Library exercises all administrative and financial powers within the main framework of rules and regulations as introduced by the Ministry. Government provides annual grants to the Library through the Ministry and decides on all fiscal and personnel matters.

The first major initiative taken by the Library in augmenting its collection development plan as well as to procure and preserve Indian printed heritage was through the enactment of Indian legal deposit legislation or Delivery of Books Act, 1954[2]. The Act, commonly referred to as DB Act was amended in 1956 to include newspapers and serials under its purview. Annual publishing of books in India during 1950s was small and below 30,000 titles, whereas by 2010 it is claimed to have exceeded 100,000 [estimated figures obtained from Federation of Indian Publishers]. The crux of the matter is National Library is missing annually a large number of Indian publications (70 per cent of annual publications) that are supposed to be received under the DB Act. The Central Reference Library (housed in the same campus) started to bring out Indian National Bibliography (INB) from 1958 as a monthly serial publication, based on the books received by the National Library under the DB Act. However, one must not lose sight of the fact that the library is in no obligation under the legal deposit act, to bring out current national bibliographies of books thus received.

The primary objective of the Act is to collect and preserve our printed heritage in every format and media, at a central repository and the National Library has been formally identified of having such status by the government of India.But the DB Act also facilitated other three 'regional' libraries in Mumbai, Chennai and Delhi as recipient libraries with the idea of making iteasier to have access to these books by people living respective regions. This decision has been found to be ineffective in the long run. Countries such as, USA, Russia (former USSR), China are much bigger countries but are having one central repository of national publications. The only major exception is the UK where five other libraries (in addition to the British Library) are being identified to claim any current publication of their choice. Moreover, in this digital age the idea of far off places, is even more to be accepted as obsolete. Secondly, the concept of administrative advantage in regional groupings of States or in distribution of other national resources on regional basis has now been proved to be only a myth. All the relevant Acts–DB Act, 1954, Press and Book Registration Act, 1867 and Copyright Act of India, 1957–required to be reviewed and updated further in the present perspective where a large majority of publications are likely to be in digital format.

Most national libraries of the world are having full responsibilities of preserving and allowing access to their collections by providing adequate indexing and other access tools, e.g., national bibliographies, subject bibliographies, annotated catalogues of special collections, many of these are now accessible online on their respective websites. We must allow the National Library for setting up National Bibliographic Division with full control of bringing out *INB* and to provide other bibliographic services covering pan-India in appropriate standardised formats, as required from time to time. By taking full advantage of technological advances supported by a group of committed well qualified staff, the library would be able to help in both improving and widening the scope of services to individuals as well as to provide back-up services to a large number of academic and public libraries in and outside the country. For example, the day Indian libraries in general adopt the same processing format for all new titles listed in *INB,* India can claim to have won half the battle in modernising our library services and systems. Without going into details one can only highlight the fact of centralised processing initiated and applied in large number of national libraries which have directly and indirectly helped respective library systems of these countries. This crucial issue was also emphasised by Uma Majumder of National library in her study[6]. We are well aware of the fact that both the CRL and *INB* are as if, linked with the DB Act by an umbilical cord that needs to be focussed and dealt with separately for a drastic revision.

ISBN/ISSN *:* In early 1980s, when India decided to join ISBN and ISSN programmes, both Federation of Indian Publishers (FIP) and the National Library declined operational responsibilities on the plea of not having adequate trained man-power and facilities. Ministry of Human Resources Development (HRD), being responsible for 'book promotion', created a small unit within National Educational Resource Centre (NERC) as a simple stop gap arrangement. The unit continues to be a section of the same ministry and is now known as ISBN Centre. In the beginning (mid-1980s), the Centre was asking all the publishers for a copy of every new book to be delivered to the Centre for allocating ISBN. Only after carrying on with this practice for over a decade, the Centre realised the mammoth task of getting adequate staff and organised enough storage space for the books thus received and worse still, where to find some readers or users. Several exhibitions of these Indian publications were organised in academic institutions. This activity was given up shortly. Entire stock of books received earlier were all been giving away to schools and colleges. Similarly, the responsibility of assigning ISSN was given to INSDOC (now part of NISCAIR, CSIR). Initially, INSDOC used to charge a fee for assigning ISSN to Indian periodical publications on receiving the first issue of a new title. Now, NISCAIR is providing ISSN free of charge. Both these two unique identification numbers are now being allocated online to publishers. Both book trade and number of libraries find it useful for online ordering, acquisition and stock control. These numbers are also being used in creating different types of bibliographical records by libraries to provide online access to various data bases.

It would be logical to merge these two activities related to Indian publications and for bibliographic control, under the overall control of the National Library as practiced in several other countries or by organisations like, FIP. One may argue why disturb a system or programme that are being carried on over three decades by two different Delhi based organisations/ units of the central government. We must accept the fact that both these codifying activities were passed on to the units to 'carry on' at a time when the National Library was not in a position of taking their genuine responsibilities for not having adequate staff strength. The present temporary arrangement of having the ISBN Centre as an appendage to the HRD Ministry needs to be put permanently under the National Library for effective coordination. This move could help in improving annual publications receipt figures of the National Library under legal deposit legislation. Today, Library has the qualified manpower and access to appropriate technologies that would allow these two Units to function independently without shifting any staff one way or the other. Existing staff serving the units shall continue to be based in Delhi, only their parent ministries will change. Career of none of the staff serving in these units will be affected by the proposed merger. On the other hand, their promotional avenues would likely to be widened considerably.

Reading Room: The main general reading room has now shifted into the new specious Bhasha Bhavan building. The old vice-regal lodge, Belvedere, is under major renovation. The old reading room though not designed for a library, had its exclusive charm and grandeur. It is believed, the old reading room after renovation with air conditioning facilities, shall have a permanent display of *'History of Indian Book'*. It is true the National Library is one of the oldest and the largest but it could not boast of having a comprehensive collection of early printing, various types of manuscripts and similar significant materials to support a permanent display on the topic in the old specious and attractive reading room. Perhaps, it would be more appropriate to allow the old reading room for the exclusive use of research scholars for special and private collections only. That will help in bringing back its old glory. The remaining area on the same floor (excluding the reading room) earlier occupied by administration section, entrance hall and the basement used to hold the book stacks, may be considered for all kinds of exhibition and displays, publications and sales, special bindery with conservation and preservation units. Rooms or chambers on upper floors may be allocated to language or similar specialised sections of the Library.

The new general reading room in Bhasha Bhavan on the first floor is specious and well lighted. The main staircase leading to reception and display area is (a) built at an awkward location and (b) climbing the steps to reach the reading room is not comfortable for senior citizens not to talk of persons with physical disabilities. There is an urgent need of erecting an escalator from the ground level, close by the staircase especially for the benefit of these categories of library users. I am sure the authorities are seriously considering of utilising the display area and the lobby not only for a more effective use but also to give this location a 'most welcome and vibrant' environmental look. There is an urgent need of adequate display of signage in all public access areas within the building. Management may have been already on the job with the help of professional interior decorators and exhibition/display experts hired on annual contract.

The National Library must take a policy decision to adopt a uniform cataloguing code (one of ISO approved standards that has a universal acceptability) both for *INB* and in-house cataloguing practices.

The National Library must follow a uniform Subject Headings List (for example, Library of Congress with modifications to suit Indian conditions);

The National Library should introduce one single set of guidelines for Romanisation for all non-Roman scripts. The effective date of this modification/modernisation process shall be publicised well in advance, announcing the effective cut-off date/s of this switch over, including the time the library would require for in-house training of staff and taking control of all other relevant management issues. Whether *INB* shall continue to record Colon Classification numbers for each title is a matter of argument.

Buildings–Underground Linkage: The three main buildings within the Belvedere campus–Bhasha Bhavan, old main building and the annexe–are all scattered over the campus area. Movement of man and material not only creates logistical hazards but also brings in unnecessary exposure to atmospheric pollution, heat and humidity. The existing practice is risky from security angle; reduces life span of documents and utterly inefficient inslowing down point to point delivery process. Now is the time for the authorities to seriously consider of linking the three main buildings through an underground tunnel while old main building is undergoing major renovation. Take for example, all the three buildings of the US Library of Congress, Washington DC are inter-connected through a specious tunnel. If this subway/tunnel is constructed, many of the crucial security issues and movement of men and material will be saved from fearful weather hazards. No doubt, the authorities are in the process of introducing soon smart card IDs both for staff and member/visitors of the Library. In addition to seminar rooms and conference hall in Bhasha Bhavan for small group meetings, the old auditorium of the National Library (annexe) needs complete over all renovation to be fully equipped with modern technological facilities for large audio-visual presentation including concerts, lectures, conferences, etc. This is considered to be an immediate need for the Library.

Scholars' Hostel: The Library provides some temporary accommodation to a few out station scholars who are new to the city and wish to stay close to the library. This facility has been running for several years but 'not found suitable' by the users/ scholars. The authorities have decided to build a new hostel with better facilities. This unique facility is unknown to many research scholars having experience of using several such libraries outside India. It is learnt, Indira Gandhi National Centre for the Arts (IGNCA), New Delhi has started offering hostel facilities to a few selected visitors, in collaboration with a five star hotel group on full payment. Authorities are surely going overboard by extending this favour to the scholarly community. It is hoped the facilities and security issues of the new hostel will satisfy all. We are well aware of the dynamics of information and communication technologies (ICT) that has been continuously reducing gaps between source of information and the user. The National Library have to take some bold policy decisions on flexible staff structure, application of appropriate technologies to keep pace with the time and bring compatibility in services with similar national libraries of the world. There are several examples of some libraries successfully providing both information and multi-media texts online on experimental basis. We hope this library will shortly reach a stage of providing such services to several outstation research scholars interested in Indian publications that will be more useful and better than what *Google/amazon/Yahoo* and other commercial online text delivery services offered online.

Publication and Research : Over the years, National Library brought out several volumes of its catalogues and two commemorative volumes narrating the historical accounts of the library. Recently, it has published a few proceedings of conferences and seminars organised by the library. The library brings out a half-yearly *Newsletter* with limited circulation. The latest issues of the *Newsletter* and a pamphlet *Reader's Guide to the National Library* are being brought out in a more attractive format which surely is a positive deviation from the old stereotype 'Indian official publications'. The *Newsletter* may please be brought out more frequently with a wider distribution network both within and outside India, preferably online as well. The National Library must have its own publication unit with a team of well qualified and trained staff with editing, designing, production and marketing background. Current practice of promoting sales and marketing of publications must not be limited to participation at national book fairs. It may be useful for the library to hire some consulting agency to develop this unit. There has to be one proper 'Sales and Display' area with modern display facilities to be located closer to the main foyer/entrance area.

Publication programme of NL may include, in addition to revised and update volumes of special catalogues, facsimile editions of rare and rich examples of outstanding quality of literary works, illuminated manuscripts, calligraphy, miniature paintings, early printing in India, Indian book binding, and picture postcards, etc., that will throw open a glimpse of its priceless varied resources; guide to special collections; research monographs; bringing out scholarly edited volumes of Indian manuscripts and many more. Scholarly research and similar high level academic activities needs to be encouraged and sponsored by the library. Earlier, several staff members were engaged in serious academic research and bibliographic activities that were later privately published and a few could not complete individual projects due to lack of encouragement or institutional support. It is the responsibility of the library authorities to identify 'quality' staff and encourage them to pursue scholarly activities that would bring credit to the institution they serve. In addition, National Library would be having specific research projects where outside scholars and library professionals could be associated. One of its primary research areas should be library and information services and systems that would be having wider scope and coverage. Very soon the Library will bring out e-publications and create data bases both online and off line (including *INB*). The job of up loading its main catalogues on its web site and reformatting a section of its older collections through digitisation are in progress. Materials received under legal deposit legislation (revised) must get priority for digitisation, over everything else, as National Library is considered to be fully responsible for the preservation and access of Indian publications for the posterity. Digitisation of non-Indian 'useful' publications shall not get preference as many such titles would likely to be digitised by similar organisations in the countries' of their origin. Some of publication unit staff must be well-qualified and trained to deal with e-publication in its entirety.

Exhibition, Display, Promotion and Publicity: Library organises both long and short term exhibitions and displays on varied themes, national issues, important occasions or celebrations. This would require scholarly approach and specialised knowledge. As these jobs are in fact part of regular activities of the library, a separate section with adequate trained manpower and supporting equipment and accessories would be required. Every national library is an integral part of total national heritage collection and preservation. It contributes significantly in nation building and heritage preservation. In today's world, a national institution that serves public at large both through direct and indirect ways and means is to have an efficient media and public relation unit. Take for example the case of the Bibliotheque Nationale, Paris and its new Tolbiac building, the benefits which it provides in terms of an enlarged cultural opportunity to transmit knowledge to the general public by means of increased public programmes, exhibitions, musical and literary events and educational services.

In line with the present practice adopted by several national libraries, e.g., Australia, Canada and the British Library and their success stories, Indian National Library may consider of adding a feature in its website inviting "Friends and Volunteers of the National Library" to get enrolled. One example, is to encourage young volunteers who would be visiting India/Kolkata and may be happy to provide help in processing several foreign language publications that have been accumulated and perhaps lying unattended, in return of providing just simple hostel accommodation for short duration. These groups may help in providing information or play an active role in raising fund or endowments/bequeathing a valuable private collection or research grants on specific topics.

National Library organises several seminars and conferences;some are related to library and information field. It holds a few lectures every year on different topics by eminent personalities of different discipline from India and abroad. The Library must widen its scope and be more active in this sphere, e.g., invite eminent scholars and specialists in different disciplines on payment, for annual memorial lectures, literary activities in all languages, book review club, film society, and several other cultural programmes and activities, both jointly and / or sponsored by an organisation of repute. A series of events, performances and musical concerts must also be a regular feature of library activities to enhance the size and composition of visitors. These invited lectures delivered and other such programmes could constitute as one of its regular publication series. There is no need now in Kolkata for the library to run a children's library as the State of West Bengal has its own public library network with children's library programme. However, children's literature, film, etc., must find their due place in the library's promotional activities.

Library staff : The image of every institution, academic or otherwise, is directly related to the staff– their professionalism and output as reflected in day to day services provided to the patrons. The Head of the institution, i.e., Director General of the National Library (DG) has the crucial role to play in every sphere of the library activities and its relationship with the users. Library staff as a unit is one of the four main components of a library: (1) Users, (2) Staff, (3) Information resources and (4) Building, equipment and other physical amenities. Being a subordinate office of the centre government, it is difficult to bring in any specific change for better or worse within the existing framework of rules and regulations that governs every institution, including the library, under the Government of India. These are being adopted and followed by the entire bureaucratic hierarchical decision making process of the system. The other major hurdle for the library is manpower recruitment procedures lies exclusively with the Union Public Service Commission and Staff Selection Commission (UPSC and SSC).

The DG (recently up graded) of the National Library would be having the right background and experience of a senior academic or a library professional who would be responsible primarily for the collection development of the library. We have no reason to disagree with the idea but keeping in view of the present condition of the library, we believe the first priority has to be given not only on his/her academic or scholarship that would surely help in collection development matters but also someone with a vision and capability of accepting the challenge of making the library to serve as the hub of library systems and services of India. His job description must include complete restructuring of staff strength together with respective job descriptions in each category/individual, within the new staff hierarchy. It is not possible to take care of the library's collection development by a single specialist scholar at the top. There must be several subject, language specialists and management experts in different fields, at the second tier, who shall be responsible as a team for overall development of the institution. It is true that since 1976 the library had a few senior library professionals who served as Director of the institution. Unfortunately, none could deliver or brought in required positive changes during their tenures of service. The existing staff structure only allow all senior executive posts, including the Director General and the two senior most library professionals, to be recruited direct through Union Public Service Commission. DG is authorised to deal with all budgetary allocation of fund. Being a subordinate office, it is bound by all procedural rules and regulations of the central government including personnel management.

Government of India could seriously consider of bringing the National Library under an autonomous public trust and allow the Board of Trustees to formulate policy and planning with full responsibility for their implementation and deal directly with all management issues. The Board of Trustees shall have the power and authority to meet its total manpower requirements. The chairperson of the Board shall be an eminent scholarly personality nominated by the government. There are several prestigious institutions of national importance that are operating under similar terms and conditions. After deciding the date of implementation of this Act, all staff members on the present pay role shall be given the option of continuing on their existing terms and condition until such time he or she reaches respective superannuation stage. Those who opted for the new management (including all future employees) shall come under the rules and service conditions as formulated from time to time by the Trust.

Selection of manpower for the National Library through the Union Public Service Commission and Staff Selection Commission has not produced effective results. One of the main shortcomings of the present selection procedures is long delay in the selection process; another limitation for the employer (the Ministry/Department/National Library) of not having any say in the final selection process. Both these factors have resulted in hiring someone with 'essential qualifications' only. Procedural delay factor of UPSC has been depriving National Library to hire the 'best suitable candidate' who shall be always on demand. Another factor that affects in getting 'new blood' due to insignificant turnover of staff due to some rigid centre government rules.

References

1. *India 2011: A Reference Annual,* Delhi, Publication Division, 127-28.
2. *India, Delivery of Books Act,1954 (amended 1956).*
3. *India,* Ministry of Culture: *Annual Report, 2009-10,* 187-88, 2010.
4. Mandal (S) and Syed Abuzar: 'Indian National Bibliography: Looking Out For Its New Era', in *National Library: NACONAL 2006,* 115-128.
5. India. Press and Registration of Books Act, 1867.
6. Majumder (Uma): '*India's National Library: Systematisation and Modernisation,* 1987, 65.

2

The National Library of India Must Act Fast

Background

The National Library (NL) in Kolkata is now in a state of flux and moving in the same pattern and pace like most other libraries in the country. It is true the library is visited daily by a large number of local readers and academics together with a handful of out station research scholars. Many of the local young readers are using this as a library of first call. The rich and varied collection of the library is the mainstay of most academic pursuits in Kolkata. In the interest of social inclusion, the library follows a simple admission procedure. The continuous downhill slide over the last several decades cannot be stopped as very little reformation was brought in by the Heads who served the library recently. None is there to hold the rein and infuse required impetus and directions so as to put it on the galloping mode with strong determination of making it to act as the hub of the nation's library and information services and systems.

To set the recovery process on, one has to go into the roots to identify the causes of this poor state of the library. It would be unfair to point a finger only towards the Department of Culture for their inconsistent policy guidelines and slow implementation machinery, nor the staff associations of the National Library for their involvement by over stepping in management issues with socio-political twist. The other party directly associated with the library is the senior management who also must share the responsibilities for bring the NL to its present state. At the same time, one must not ignore the mute role of the library professional organisations and users groups of the library, who by acting as lobbyists with some support from the media, could have kept a watchful eye and bring moral pressure on all the stakeholders. If we look at the management structure of an effective national library systems of the United Kingdom, one cannot miss the point of noticing their national library has acquired the recognition of being the apex body for national knowledge storage and handling systems and a guiding factor for all research and developmental activities related to library and information services. Sadly enough, this is not the role what our library professional think tank is considering for the National Library.

The National Library is perhaps the weakest link within Indian library systems. The most recent thoughts on Indian library and information services are being reflected in the ten Recommendations of the National Knowledge Commission (2006)[1] which presented a programme of actions with 2020 as the projected target schedule for achieving the goals. Its Working Group on Libraries (NKC-WGL) did not focus on the role of the National Library, in the proposed library network development. For some reasons, best known to the Group, it avoided dealing with the National Library exclusively. There have been many national and international conferences and seminars held over the last few decades, organised by the National Library and by other organisations on topics closely relevant to it. Let us not go for checking the results of follow-up actions, if any, on the long list of pious resolutions or recommendations adopted in these academic or professional forums. Only very recently, the Library organised a National Conference on the National Library[2], (NACONAL, 2006) and brought out a voluminous publication of the papers presented at the conference. This publication and the NKC-WGL recommendations will give us some idea of the trends of thoughts of our library professionals. The National Library and the Indian library professionals, individuals and groups, must act together to pursue with the policy makers for implementation of some of the recommendations within a reasonable time schedule (2020).

Rajiv Gandhi, former Prime Minister, while laying the foundation stone in 1989 of Bhasa Bhavan, the latest building complex added to the National Library of India, expressed his desire to see the National Library of India at par with other national libraries of the world, keeping in view of its massive information flow, its storage and retrieval. Dr Manmohan Singh, Prime Minister of India (2004-2014), declared the formation of National Knowledge Commission at the CII Partnership Summit, 2005 at the National Library campus on 12th January, 2005 emphasised that the National Knowledge Commission would be a catalyst in setting ambitious knowledge targets and enabling agencies to attain them. The first of the five specific agenda items he stressed was, 'to increase access to knowledge for public benefit. It is now over eight years since the Chairman of NKC submitted a set of ten specific recommendations to the Prime Minister on 7th December, 2006, to act upon for the up-gradation of library and information services.

On 8th October, 2004 Bhasa Bhavan was declared open to the public by the then Minister of Culture. This additional space of over 40,000 sq meters is surely of great help to the library to widen its activities by providing more shelf space to house its valuable reading materials and some additional reading space for the users, in a more comfortable air-conditioned environment. But over the last few years all its developmental and modernisation activities have come to a halt due to critical shortage of staff at every level. About 50 per cent of the posts are lying vacant due to superannuation and other reasons, but there is no new move by the government to fill up these vacancies. Whenever a Director (recently upgraded to Director General) completes his tenure there is always a stop-gap Director of RRRLF to take charge till a new incumbent takes over. This arrangement is going on for over the last 25 years.

This critical staff situation of the National Library is not known to many people in rest of India. There were of course a few protest marches with banners and loud-speakers on roads of Kolkata, some posters placed near the front entrance, by the staff and employees associations or a few editorial comments in a few local newspapers or in professional journals which failed to create any ripple within the concerned Ministry of the Government of India. National print and electronic media, have little time and space to cover the services provided or not provided by this cultural centre of national importance. Indian cinema and television, both documentary and entertainment channels have totally neglected the world of books and libraries.

One must also bring out the present crisis faced by another library—the Central Secretariat Library, New Delhi (CSL), the second largest library under the direct control of the same Ministry. CSL is also over 100 years old that holds another valuable collection of research materials. This library has lost nearly half of its sanctioned professional staff over the last ten years. Tulsi Sadan, its regional language unit, has been closed down and more than half of the library's older collections have been 'disposed of ' to make room to accommodate ministerial staff. No attempt has been made so far to fill up these vacancies and the library is being asked to 'carry on' by hiring a few 'short-term trainees' with fresh LIS back ground, at regular intervals. Now with the recently introduced strict security regulations, CSL has lost most of the regular readers and research scholars who are 'not centre government employees'. The Ministry has to seriously consider of moving this library out of the Shastri Bhavan complex. Perhaps it would be better still, if this library is merged with another local reference library of the National Social Science Documentation Centre under ICSSR, fully funded by the Ministry of HRD, whose collection and users group would ideally complement each other.

We consider it right to point a finger at the library and information professional organisations whose primary role is to act as a watch dog but consistently failed to take up these national issues seriously with the bureaucratic and political decision making process at the national level. Strangely, Indian mass media is least bothered to highlight this poor state of affairs and inefficient library service, where academics and intellectual community are the real sufferers thereby bringing in a loss to the nation.

Positive Moves

1. The recently published volume containing papers presented at the NACONAL 2006 by the National Library, listed a few papers worth serious follow up actions particularly by the library management and professional organisations. There is however, some move by the Ministry of Culture by organising a meeting of the stakeholders on 8th February, 2009 with the purpose of setting up the National Mission for Libraries (NML), as recommended by NKC. The minutes of the meeting are yet to be made public.
2. By organising NACONAL, 2006, the library attempted to obtain different viewpoints and suggestions, on its future course, from a large section library professionals in the country, and to have close interactions with them, is surely a positive move. To supplement this, library must look at the large amount of documentation available on web sites of different national libraries of the world, followed by directly interacting with some of them on specific issues of mutual interest. This vast back up information resources will help the National Library to prepare a draft action plan, both on long (20 years) and short (five years) term, indicating projected targets and goals to achieve under separate Heads of activities.
3. It is true the library is presently short of quality management personnel. Board should also consider of hiring services of some recognised consultancy agency

who could be asked to conduct a comprehensive survey of the Library users' groups, their pattern of use, what they want and their expectations of quality and level of services. This may sound unprecedented to many of us. Of late, several centre government organisations are involving private professional groups and individuals for some specific services for their specialised management skills. Armed with this the Board may assign a group of management experts to prepare a blue print on 'New Policy and Planning' which needs to be widely circulated before drawing a plan of action.

If a strategy is needed for the National Library to meet the demands of the twenty first century we must take some calculated drastic measures that will justify investment of resources provided by the taxpayers. Recently, the British Library launched a major consultation with its users with its '*New Strategic Directions for the British Library*'.[4] There were over 5,000 responses, which largely endorsed the themes of working in collaboration and partnership, increasing the understanding of users needs, widening access to collections and services and accelerating the library's *e*-strategy. But to get a pan-India sample of 5,000 users for our National Library is a different matter altogether because very few out station users visit or get any direct service from the National Library, Kolkata. There is a huge gap between what the National Library is expected, compared to its present coverage, and why no remedial action has been taken to reduce the gaps is never been questioned. Moreover, it is not that we are not aware of these shortcomings in services of the National Library as there are several government appointed committees' and commissions' reports spelt them out with suggestions for improvements.

Role and Strategy

It is perhaps because of this uncertainty the National Knowledge Commission, Working Group for Libraries avoided to identify the distinctive role of National Library of India within a holistic Indian library and information systems and services. Question may also be raised by a few, why go for another report on the National Library? This proposed study is to be based on real life users' survey undertaken and conducted under direct supervision of the National Library; not imposed upon it by some 'eminent scholar/bureaucrat'. The most recent report on the National Library is of a high-powered committee headed by Prof Satish Chandra (1994-95). The revised National Library Act of 1976[5] (partially implemented) also included many significant modifications to improve its management. The most significant reason is that with the passage of time and pace at which information and communication technologies are influencing information storage, access and retrieval our National Library must make the right moves after clearly defining its role and identifying the means to reach its goal. Rapid and significant developments are taking place in all three segments of librarianship over the last four decades–(i) Collection development of information resources, (ii) Customers services (including cataloguing, education, reference services and inter-library loans) and (iii) Management and Marketing. The library has to be active on all the fronts and needs a little push and encouragement from all of us.

The British Experience

It is significant and also relevant to record that the British Library, the US Library of Congress have been constantly reviewing their role for updating the services. National Library has got some additional space (Bhasa Bhavan) after making demands for it in early 1960s. Though the 1976 Act was not implemented due to various reasons, the government took the opportunity of bringing in some changes in the administrative structure of staff at the higher level. Satish Chandra Committee report fell short of identifying library's future role in: the research information cycle to outline its strategies for research in science, technology and medicine in higher education and industry; the social sciences in higher education; the practitioner communities; research in the arts and humanities in higher education and the creative industries. There is a strong and urgent need to redefine its role and strategies. The British Library[6] redefined its role in 2005, "The library must address and define the strategic priorities of enriching the user's experience, building digital research library, transforming search and navigation, growing and managing the national collection, qualitative improvement of its staff and guaranteeing financial sustainability."

There has always been a conflict of interest and in approach between librarian and management on utilising grants from public funding agencies on the value of library–what return in real economic terms, the tax-payers get for the investment made on a library? Librarian's answer, sometimes supported by the academic and research community, has always been subjective based on qualitative analysis–'it is a service to the public, like education, health care, sports, etc.' There are a few recent case studies on some specific services of a particular library based on some analytical data to justify the viability of that service on monetary terms. What attracted me most is the British Library's recent publication, *Measuring Our Value*, based on a survey conducted by designing carefully a questionnaire. Data analysis was carried on a method known as contingent valuation method (CVM) exploited by the Nobel Prize-winning economists, Kenneth Arrow and Robert Solow to determine the direct and indirect value–economic, culture, social and intellectual–added by the British Library to the nation. Over 2000 people were asked:

- How much they would be willing to pay for the library's continued existence;
- What was the minimum payment they would be willing to accept to forgo the library's existence;
- How much they invested in terms of time and money to make use of the library;

- How much they would have to pay to use alternatives to the library, if such alternatives could be found.

The conclusions were that the total value each year of the British Library was in terms of British sterling pound, 363 million (of which 304 million was indirect value and 59 million direct value); for every one pound sterling of public funding the British Library received annually, 4.40 pound was generated for the UK economy; and if the British Library did not exist, the UK would lose 280 million of economic value per annum. Survey helped the British Library to prioritise its strategies on their staff development. In 2004, the library introduced a radical competency-based performance system which was intended to be eventually linked to performance pay.

There is no comparison between the services provided by the present British Library and National Library of India. Historically, however, National Library of India was established on the model of the British Library (formerly British Museum Library) and it continued to be providing similar kind of satisfactory service to the users till the end of 1960s.

Action Plan

The National Library Act of 1976 proposed to declare the library as an autonomous body which was not acceptable to the employees of the library. In a recent paper presented at the NACONAL, 2006, Dasgupta (2006)[8], former Librarian/PLIO of the National Library came out with ten recommendations for the betterment of the library. The first item of her recommendations is, 'the National Library needs to be changed to...a more autonomous institution within the government structure'. Under the sixth item she recommends, "The major requirement is to actually make the library 'exclusive' in every respect." It is not clear what this exclusiveness will cover. At the end of these recommendations, she mentioned, "I must share... that these suggestions are not mine but that of the National Library staff, who are now mentally and professionally ready to take on new responsibilities to make this library a major institution in the region." In NKC-WGL[9] recommendations, she as chairperson, avoided to recommend any specific future role of the National Library within the total Indian library scenario. The reality is the Ministry of Culture has taken some steps for implementing the first two recommendations of the NKC–WGL. Hence, it would not be surprising if the National Library is left out of the loop of the future growth pattern of Indian library network. Dasgupta[10] approved of the National Library's new initiative to focus more on eastern and north-eastern states of India in terms of acquisition of resource materials and to help in training library staff of the regions. This special initiative was taken under the instructions of the Ministry of Culture. This may be a strategic move but this is nothing more than a short sighted approach by the government. Location of the National Library in today's context is immaterial as digital and communication technologies shall allow anyone to have direct access not only to its own resources but also any other information resources in digital format without even visiting the local information centre.

As a follow-up to National Knowledge Commission's recommendations, the government (Ministry of Culture) recently called a meeting of the stakeholders of Indian libraries. The government has set up the National Mission on Libraries (NML) which is believed to be in the process of drawing an action plan for the government to take a formal move for preparing the Census of Indian libraries and preparing an outline of having the Indian Digital Library, as recommended by NKC. These are some positive moves while the rest of NKC recommendations may be left with the proposed NML to deal, and/or other developmental activities to enlarge the size and composition of library users in India. National Library must be a critical partner to be represented in NML. What is required of the National Library is to actively participate and take major share of responsibilities to help the Mission in fulfilling its task. We guess, the ministry will provide the requisite support by allowing the National Library to hire competent staff in adequate number.

We must start with a clean slate instead of bickering on the past. Things are to change sooner than later in making the National Library resources easily accessible to anybody at every corner of India with the newly available information and communication technology. Fortunately, the library has taken some positive moves to adopt these technologies, though at a very slow pace. One of the main reasons for this slow progress is severe shortage of trained manpower and lack of appropriate focus on the goals, at the management level. No resource is more critical to any library or information centre than its own group of qualified manpower. The quality of their training, appropriateness of that training to existing and changing conditions, and their respective attitude towards the patron can make or break programmes and provide satisfaction or discontent among a large section of the users.

Under the present system, all the posts are to be filled up through UPSC and Staff Selection Commission only, is itself a complicated long drawn process. With the implementation of the National Library Act of 1976 (with modification) and the proposed revised Delivery of Books Act, the National Library Board could be authorised to take over complete responsibility of hiring all categories of staff for the library.

Another sensitive issue is the future relationship of Central Reference Library (CRL) with the National Library which is kept hanging over the last sixty odd years. Original proposal was to move CRL eventually to Delhi after a suitable building is constructed at the proposed site earmarked in Lutyens' Delhi plan, opposite to the National Museum. Government has finally gave up the idea of shifting CRL or the National Library to Delhi under pressure from various corners and the new under construction Jawaharlal Nehru Bhavan on the site is meant for various units (including the departmental library) of the Ministry of External Affairs. CRL is ideally suited to act as the fully automated bibliographic division of the National Library thereby avoiding duplication of processing of books and other items received by the Library under the DB Act. National Library must come out with a concrete proposal of unification of CRL. The issue of seniority in hierarchies within the staff of the two libraries should not stop any longer of serving a larger national cause. This is not uncommon within the central government of merging staff of two units of a department.

Let us hope the ministry will do its best to get the revised draft DB Act passed by the Parliament very soon. If the present National Library Advisory Board could make a concerted effort to get over these two hurdles at the earliest with the help of the ministry, then only we can ask the National Library to bring out a fully automated online national bibliography of international compatibility in terms of service and standards. The impact of this will be noticeable in many sectors. Manpower wasted in cataloguing all the new Indian publications once by CRL for bringing out INB issues and again by the NL before shelving the books followed by their use by the readers. Available technology will help in bringing out INB using the vernacular scripts at least for the title and author (in addition to Romanisation), and English for the descriptive part of each catalogue entry. All libraries in India shall be authorised to download INB catalogue entries or from NL database. This centralised cataloguing of all Indian publication in all languages (in original scripts) shall save a huge amount of manpower by the libraries that can be utilised for providing additional services to a wider readership. There are about 200 plus library schools attached to different universities producing over 10,000 professional librarians annually, of which more than half of these remain either unemployed or under-employed for several years. The country will save a big amount from this wastage of young talents that could be diverted to some more productive employment channels.

Another vital issue the National Library must take up immediately is to set up a consortium for creating a comprehensive National Digital Library of Indian (NDLI) for reformatting if required, all Indian publications (new and old). This collection shall include all Indian *e*-publications and selected rare materials of distinction including items considered both priceless and having considerable qualitative value. One can add many others to this list. The main objective of NDLI is to retain all digitised texts of library holdings of Indian printed and other resource materials that are worth preservation for the posterity, and make them accessible globally for research. Many Indian libraries are having their own digitalisation units and/or subscribed/procured materials of research value in digitised format. In the field of science and technology, there is some cooperative move by IITs, IIMs and IISc to create INDEST and Vidyanidhi with UGC-INFLIBNET support. In addition, there are many other libraries, which are active in this area, including CSL and National Library. We also had several International and national conferences and seminars, workshops on this topic, including the big 'Million books digital library project'. But all these activities are not focused to a single goal of developing India's own National Digital Library. This is an exclusive responsibility of the National Library; it must take the initiative and coordinate the whole project to avoid duplication and also avoid waste of tax-payers money. We cannot and must not leave this job of coordination to any other institution or library as is clearly demonstrated by the major national libraries of the world.

References

1. National Knowledge Commission, Working Group on Libraries (2006), *Recommendations.*
2. National Conference on the National Library (2006), Kolkata, *The National Library: An intellectual resource (NACONAL 2006*).

3. *Ibid., The National Library: An Intellectual Resource (NACONAL 2006).*
4. British Library (2001), *The New Strategic Directions For The British Library,* pp.21-24.
5. India. *National Library Act, 1976.*
6. British Library (2005), *Redefining The Library, British Library's Strategy 2005-2008,* London, The British Library.
7. British Library (2004), *Measuring Our Value*; results of an independent economic impact study commissioned by the British Library to measure the direct and indirect value to the UK economy. London, British Library.
8. Kalpana Dasgupta, India's National Library: Present Organisational Set-up And Future Requirements; *in The National Library of India: An Intellectual Resource. (NACONAL 2006),* pp. 355-357.
9. National Knowledge Commission, Working Group on Libraries (2006), *Recommendations.*
10. National Conference on the National Library, *The National Library: An Intellectual Resource (NACONAL, 2006*), p. 353.

3

Indian Legal Deposit Legislation and its Impact on the National Library

Legal Deposit Legislation

In 1981, UNESCO published a study prepared by Jean Lunn, *Guidelines for Legal Deposit Legislation* (Lunn, 1981). It is over 30 years since his study was published. Many countries have amended or significantly rewritten their legal deposit laws (Germany, Indonesia, and Norway in 1990, France in 1992, Sweden in 1994, Canada in 1995, South Africa in 1997, Denmark in 1998 and Japan and Finland in 2000, the United Kingdom in 2003). Others are in the process of doing so (Australia, India, Slovenia, Spain, Switzerland). The forms of intellectual and artistic expression have grown in different dimensions. New published media have been developed and electronic publications are now an integral part of many national publishing heritages.

UNESCO was under pressure to bring out a revised edition of the *Guidelines* in order to review the impact of it on other countries and to incorporate new forms of publishing, such as electronic publications. The new revised and updated edition of the *Guidelines of Legal Deposit Legislation* by Jules Lariviere (2000) is found to be a useful tool. The relevant Indian Act, Delivery of Books Act, 1954 (revised 1956 to include newspapers and periodicals), has been under the scanner since shortly after it was put into application and over the last five decades the National Library, Kolkata and the three other recipient regional public libraries (Connemara Public Library, Chennai, Central

Library, Town Hall, Mumbai and Delhi Public Library, Delhi), and especially the publishing world directly involved with it, expressed concern and drew the attention of the Government of India to its limitations and ineffectiveness. The National Library, Federation of Indian Publishers (FIP) and several professional library organisations discussed its drawbacks and recommended revision or specific amendments of the act at various seminars, conferences and other forums. The Ministry of Culture, the concerned agency of the Government of India, set up several committees to deal with the matter. The *Recommendations Of The National Knowledge Commission and its Working Group on Libraries* (National Knowledge Commission, 2006) is completely silent on this and other national library related issues. It would be most appropriate to draw attention to an article by Bandopadhyay (2000), former Director of the National Library, which is exhaustive enough with a complete planof action for the concerned ministry to initiate the revision process at the earliest opportunity. As a follow up, the ministry took some steps to obtain the views of other stakeholders, including academics, library user groups and senior library professionals. Based on these suggestions/recommendations a revised draft bill on this issue was prepared in 2006 but has yet to be approved by the ministry.

Role of the Legal Deposit Act

In simple terms, Legal Deposit is a statutory obligation which requires that any organisation, commercial or public, and any individual producing any type of documentation in multiple copies, be obliged to deposit one or more copies with some recognised national institution(s). It is important to make sure that legal deposit legislation covers all kinds of published material, that is, material generally produced in multiple copies and 'offered to the public regardless of the means of transmission'. Public distribution could mean 'performance' or 'display' for example a radio or television programme could be considered as 'published' for legal deposit purposes when it has been broadcast. Within the electronic publications environment, it should be noted that a 'one copy item', such as a database stored on one server, could be subject to the legal deposit requirement since it is made available to the public through a technology enabling the public to read, hear or view the material (Lariviere, 2000, pp. 3-4). Most countries rely on a legal instrument of some sort in order to ensure the comprehensiveness of their national deposit collection. In all countries, with a legal deposit system, 'published material' would naturally include books, periodicals, newspapers, microforms, sheet music, maps, brochures, pamphlets, etc. In some countries audio-visual material (sound recordings, films, videos, etc.) is also subject to legal deposit, and there are several countries where electronic publications are also included in the legislation, but they have done this in different ways; some have excluded online electronic publications because of the numerous unsolved technical problemsrelated to their acquisition and preservation, problems related to ever changing technological scenarios.

Legal deposit legislation serves a clear national public policy interest by ensuring comprehensive acquisition, recording, preservation of, and access to, a nation's published heritage. The role of a legal deposit system is to ensure the development of a national collection of published material in various formats. It should also support the compilation and publication of the national bibliography in order to ensure bibliographic control over a comprehensive deposit collection. In addition, effective legal deposit legislation guarantees to citizens and researchers within the country and abroad, access to a research collection of the national published material. Countries are developing many different models, but are clearly unable to keep pace with the massive changes and challenges related to the deposit of intangible publications. The UK Department of National Heritage (1997) brought out a consultative paper on current legal deposit issues, based on a questionnaire which identified several pertinent issues and posed a number of specific questions to which responses were sought from individuals and organisations. This document could also help the Indian group and the government agencies in formulating the revised DB Act.

Profile of Indian Book Publishing

Before we deal with the Indian Delivery of Books Act, let us first look at the present trends in book publishing in India. Over the last four decades, a large majority of English-language publishing has concentrated in and around the capital, Delhi. The city is also a major centre of Hindi publishing industry. The rapid growth of higher education from the 1960s, and the pressure build-up within the faculties due to the University Grants Commission's policy of 'publish or perish', resulted in an increase in the publication of research monographs. India is one of the few countries where theses and dissertations submitted for Ph.D. and other similar higher postgraduate degrees,in the humanities and social sciences particularly, are published as a routine matter, whereas in science and technology this would be a rare phenomenon.

There is no reliable source of annual book publishing data in India or any comprehensive list of Indian publishers in different languages. Malhotra (2010), an established publisher in English and Hindi, claimed there to be 15,000-20,000 publishing houses, mostly run by individuals or as a single family business. According to Vinutha Mallya (2011), senior editor of Mapin Publishing, India is the sixth largest publishing industry in the world with annual growth of 15-20 per cent; the third largest publisher of books in English (around 90,000 to 100,000 books are published annually and there are about 19,000 publishers in the country); in addition, 60 per cent of global publishing outsourcing is based in India.

This growth trend is noticeable only from the 1970s onwards when book trade turnover increased gradually due to the numerical growth of educational and research institutions at every level. As we look back a few decades, the demand for English books grew fast in libraries of newly established universities, research institutions and other academic centres. Individual buyers of books constitute only a small percentage. Bulk of the titles was imported from English-speaking countries, mostly from the UK and USA based publishing houses. This book import business is largely handled by a few Delhi based book importers and distributors. Vendors collect new titles from the distributors to supply these 'on approval' to libraries. These vendors or library suppliers, having direct contacts on a day-to-day basis with the researchers and faculty members who are the actual selectors in all educational institutions, get requests to publish research monographs from faculty members. Many of them grabbed these offers on their own terms thereby joining the exclusive club of publishers. We now find several of these vendors are retail bookshop owners, library suppliers and also publishers, all in one.

The Act, commonly referred to as DB Act, was amended in 1956 to include newspapers and serials under its purview (Delivery of Books Act, 1954). Annual publishing of books in India during the 1950s was small and below 30,000 titles, whereas by 2010 it is claimed to have exceeded 100,000 (estimated figure obtained from the Federation of Indian Publishers in the absence of any official data from any reliable source) with a substantial increase in the coverage of subjects such as science and technology. In a recent annual report of the Ministry of Culture (2010), the National Library claimed to have received 29,875 publications under the DB Act which happens to be only 30 per cent of the estimated total publications as indicated by senior executives of the library in several professional forums. It was also being pointed out in such gatherings that the other three recipient libraries under this Act, in Chennai, Delhi and Mumbai, received even less during the same period. It is worth noting that this was claimed to be the highest figure ever reached by the library 'due to a special drive' (National Library, Kolkata, 2007).

UNESCO Statistical Yearbook is silent on the number of books published annually or the number of libraries in India over the last several decades, although India is one of the major contributors and an active member of this international body. This sad state of affairs was obviously reached, and continues to be, due to the simple negligence of all concerned. In most other countries annual publication figures are provided by organisations declared as recipients under the legal deposit or copyright legislation of the country.

There must be several reasons for the library to reach such a state and to argue, we guess, the limitations of the DB Act cannot be the primary cause. Rigid administrative and fiscal rules and regulations adopted by the library to operate under the supervision of the ministry are surely crucial but not the only causes of the bottleneck in its growth process. The crux of the matter is that the National Library has never received the bulk of Indian publications under the DB Act. We do not know all who are claimed to be Indian publishers. A sizeable number of them are ignorant of DB Act obligations. It is also a fact that the number of 'one time author-publishers' is also very high (15 per cent-20 per cent), especially in vernacular languages. The National Library together with the Central Reference Library committed to bring out *Indian National Bibliography (INB)* based on the books received under the DB Act, similar in format to the *British National Bibliography (BNB*). However, neither the British Library (formerly British Museum Library) nor the Indian National Library is under any obligation under their respective legal deposit acts to bring out national bibliographies of books thus received. Rules and policies adopted are working smoothly for the British Library but similar regulations unexpectedly failed to work in our case. Bandhopadhyay points out 'one has to keep in mind the fact that default in UK is an exception rather than general rule unlike in India'.

The provision of a penalty for default in the DB Act of Rs 50.00 (one US$) sounds just notional. Either revise it to a figure, for example Rs 1,000 or four–five times the actual market price of one copy, whichever is higher, or better still, make it voluntary, and hope for the best. The reason for suggesting the latter provision is to avoid the highly cumbersome and built-in procedural delay within the legal system. The National Library to date has not taken any legal action against any publishers for defaulting. In USA, a penalty clause is not mentioned as the legal deposit provision is covered under the country's copyright Acts. It is because of this factor that legal deposit provision is more effective and acceptable to authors and publishers of this country.

It would be more realistic to suggest that under the revised Act, the National Library shall receive one copy of every Indian 'publication' and the three other regional repository libraries in Chennai, Delhi and Mumbai shall have the right of receiving free all current publications in their respective regional languages only. The current practice of demanding four copies of every publication to be delivered free of cost, to each of these four libraries (including the National Library) failed to meet our expectations. This is in addition to the publishers having to comply with the demands of different state central libraries under the Press and Registration of Books Act 1867. Moreover, a large volume of these books and other publications thus received, especially publications in languages that are not commonly used in some regions, are usually being 'dumped' or just temporarily stored as these are of 'no use' to the library. This is a colossal wastage of national resource. In addition, it would not be cost effective to have these so to say 'unused books' (four copies of each) routinely processed, to provide costly storage space and also to maintain them for posterity in four regional libraries. The National Library should receive one copy for preservation and access only, and create bibliographic records for the benefit of all stakeholders.

There are several categories of publications, for example, in the English, Hindi, Sanskrit and Urdu (EHSU) languages that find several users in all the other three regions. Let us accept the real time scenario in terms of availability and accessibility of both metadata and texts through the availability of information and communication technologies (ICT) within library systems and services. Bibliographic data for publications received by the National Library under legal deposit legislation will be accessible to others from *INB* and the National Library catalogue/database online. These three libraries should buy one copy of all selected books in EHSU languages from any local vendor/publisher. Additional annual spending by the three libraries on this account should be reimbursed from a special annual central government grant. This proposed model is based on the legal deposit system of the United Kingdom, where the British Library receives one copy of every publication and the other five legal deposit libraries (National Library of Wales, Aberystwyth, the National Library of Scotland, Edinburgh, the Bodleian Library, University of Oxford, Cambridge University Library and Trinity College Dublin), operating through the Agency for the Legal Deposit Libraries based in Edinburgh, are each entitled to claim a copy of every published work, according to their own selection policies.

Table 1: Books In Indian Languages Received In The National Library

Language	*NL/DB Act*		*INB*	*Average*
	2007-08	*2008-09*	*(2010)*	*Cost*
Assamese	97	35	337	
Bengali	991	1463	2189	
English	5756	5385	5530	830
Gujarati	127	348	476	
Hindi	2370	1722	1237	450
Kannada	687	600	877	
Malayalam	1500	1200	866	
Marathi	1400	1351	1341	
Oriya	2661	52	750	
Punjabi	602	576	000	
Sanskrit	112	287	111	350
Tamil	3685	2526	1186	
Telugu	248	145	406	
Urdu	521	304	292	300
Total	**20757**	**15994**	**15598**	

We made an attempt to get some estimation of the annual cost of books purchased by the three regional libraries that were published in these four (EHSU) 'common languages'. The revised provision in the act will also bring some savings in terms of time and resources, as a lesser number of books are to be dealt with by the regional libraries. Sooner rather than later (within a decade or so), it will be a reality to make a digital copy of an Indian publication available online by the National Library from its own stock to an individual or a library within or outside the country. The technology is already at the experimental stage at various levels. Slowly and gradually, a large number of Indian publications will be brought out in e-format only which will also change our current perception of borrowing or consulting a 'book' from a conventional library. Until we reach that stage in India (20 years), as the transitional period we shall have to carry on with both the systems as we now have both bullock carts as well as BMW 7 e-series cars on our roads for transportation. Indian library systems will take a longer path and take time to switch over to reach this goal. Moreover, any change in our library 'modernisation' programme will be fully dependent on the application of technological innovations, thus resulting in the inevitable acceptance of a never ending process. Thomas Abhram (2011) in a recent article said, 'e-books will be hugely cheaper with the removal of paper and inventory costs... All things taken into account, physical books in print format are certainly not going away during a decade or two. And e-books, from a publishing point of view, are a "consummation devoutly to be wished".' We in India, specially the National Library, are to continue dealing with physical books for several decades together with information resources available in e-books and/or any other format.

The figures quoted above (Table 1) under books received by the National Library under the DB Act during 2007-08 and 2008-09 and those listed under *INB* for 2010 (CRL) were obtained from the respective libraries by personal request. A paper presented at the National Conference on the National Library as an Intellectual Resource 2006 by Mandal and Syed Abuzar indicated the National Library received about 20,000 books annually during 1990-2002. They claimed the library received about 30,000 during 2005-06 due to a special drive and a similar number of volumes during 2010-11, as recorded in the annual report of the Ministry of Culture. Unfortunately, we could not get a breakdown of the figures under each language for the 29,875 books received during 2005-06 nor the figures for books listed in *INB* during 2009 and 2011. The noticeable difference in figures of Oriya books received during 2007–08 and 2008–09 was believed to be due to some special efforts made by the language specialist concerned during 2007.[7]

If these revised guidelines are adopted in our legal deposit act (now under revision) by taking over by the central exchequer of the extra burden on the book fund of the three regional libraries, for books published and selected in these four specific

---

7. The average cost of recently published books in English, Hindi, Sanskrit and Urdu (EHSU) languages has been worked out from a sample of books purchased by University of Delhi, Central Library, Central Secretariat Library and the US Library of Congress Book Procurement Centre in Delhi. We made here an estimation of the annual additional grant to be provided by central government to support the three regional libraries (in Chennai, Delhi and Mumbai) under the proposed revised legal deposit legislation. The three libraries are entitled, under the law, to receive free of cost one copy of a book published in the respective regional languages. It is estimated that each library would selectively acquire per year about 30,000 new Indian publications (10,000 EHSU titles + 20,000 in the respective regional languages) out of about 90,000 published annually. That means, central government would reimburse annually the cost of 30,000 books in EHSU languages where the average cost of a set of four EHSU books is Rs 2,000, that is Rs 60 million in total. In addition, another Rs 10 million would be required to cover annual subscription costs of EHSU periodicals and newspapers. Thus we reach an estimated figure of Rs 70 million or seven crore (add another 10 per cent annually for inflation). These figures are being presented to get some idea of the extra cost we propose to pass on to the central government exchequer.

languages, perhaps we could expect improved cooperation from the publishing fraternity in fulfilling their responsibilities towards the provisions of the revised act. To keep a balance on 'free delivery' the group of publishers bringing out EHSU language publications are to supply two free copies, like all other publishers, one to the National Library and the other to Parliament Library. Indian publishers may legitimately expect to find *INB* to be an up-to-date and comprehensive tool to serve the community in a more effective way.

Central Reference Library (CRL), Kolkata

The library started in 1955, is situated within the National Library Campus and is primarily responsible for the compilation of *Indian National Bibliography (INB)* since 1958, based on the books and other publications received by the National Library under the Delivery of Books Act, 1954 (rev. 1956). This library was supposed to find a permanent home in Delhi which may never happen. Attempts were made during the 1970s and 1980s to merge CRL with the National Library but were stalled by the staff associations of the two libraries.

Indian National Bibliography (INB)

It started in 1958 following the *British National Bibliography (BNB)* format. To overcome the complexity of multi-script languages, it adopted Romanisation of all scripts with the descriptive part of each entry in English. This has created problems for many who are not familiar with Roman script or the English language. The job of printing *INB* monthly issues was given exclusively to the Government of India Press in Kolkata that failed to realise, from the beginning, the importance of maintaining the production and delivery schedule. After years of persuasion by CRL, the ministry allowed printing of *INB* through alocal private press. Every title received by the National library under the BD Act is first acknowledged by the Library then sent to CRL, where it is catalogued once according to *INB* practices and then sent back to the National Library for re-cataloguing according to its own specified rules, followed by due processing for storage. These long drawn administrative procedural factors and duplication of the cataloguing process are claimed to be a major cause of delay from the date of receipt of the publication to the time itsrecord is found in *INB*, followed by making it available to readers. The National Library takes its own time, sometimes nearly two years, to allow access to the books received under the DB Act. The important job of promotion and marketing of the *INB* has not been given much importance by the concerned authorities. Adaptation of appropriate technologies at different levels by the management of the library, and to provide smooth access to resources have continuously been lagging.

Proposals

The title of the revised act should be 'Delivery of Publications (National Library) Act'.

The definition of Publications shall include – all printed documents, such as books, periodicals, serials and newspapers, e-publications including audio books, CD books, DVDs and digital online publications and/or any other reformatted or original document produced for commercial distribution, for example microform documents.

Only one copy of all publications shall be delivered free of cost, direct to the National Library of India (or at an address specified by the Library). The act should also make adequate provision for the three regional libraries based in Chennai, Delhi and Mumbai to receive one copy of all publications in their respective regional languages, free of cost direct from the publishers. The publishers of English, Hindi, Sanskrit and Urdu (EHSU) languages shall send one copy of each of their publications to the Parliament Library.

One copy of selected current publications in four 'common' languages (English, Hindi, Sanskrit and Urdu) shall be purchased by the three regional libraries from funds specially allocated annually by the central government.

Any publication, irrespective of its origin and format, imported into India for commercial purposes in more than one hundred copies, must be covered under the revised Legal Deposit Act.

Similarly titles published simultaneously in several countries (including India), irrespective of their origin of production/ printing shall be treated as Indian publications.

The new revised act must allow the National Library some discretionary power to discard or offer as a gift to other institutions some materials received under the act.

Central Reference Library (CRL) shall not have its separate identity any longer. Total CRL activities and staff shall be merged with the National Library. The backbone of CRL is its editorial staff, which shall be merged with the different language sections of the library. The existing separate cadres of the two libraries may continue until the superannuation of each staff member; all newly-recruited staff shall be under a single staff cadre. This mergershall not affect any of the existing staff in their emoluments or other terms of service as recommended by the Sixth Pay Commission. The proposed Act of cadre merger is not unique within central government.

Indian National Bibliography (INB) shall continue to be published as hard copy until such time as it will be required to switch over to online electronic format. There may be some need to bring out *INB* in both hard and soft copies for a short period of time.

INB could be brought out in four parts: 1. EHSU languages, 2. Eastern Indian, 3. Southern Indian and 4. Western Indian language fascicules.

It would meet a long-standing demand, if each entry in vernacular languages/scripts could also include author and title only in the original scripts. Technology for such a modification is available in India.

Press and Registration of Books Act, 1867 (PR Act)

This Act is in a way the first legal deposit legislation in India. It is a regulatory act enacted by the British government, with the primary intentionof keeping a tab on the local printing press. It is to regulate printing presses and newspapers with the provision of receiving copies of all such items under the Act. One copy of every book and other material printed in India was sent to England. Printed material in different Indian languages and subjects thus received was retained partly in the India Office Library and Records (now merged with the British Library) under the Secretary of State, and the rest in the British Museum Library. The two libraries produced catalogues of printed books received under this act, in different languages. Both these libraries have now been merged to constitute the bulk of the South Asian core collections of the present day British Library. Many of the books printed or published by different state governments and corporate bodies, including books of general interest, were retained by the India Office Library, the rest were passed on to the British Museum. The British Museum in turn retained only the books considered to be of 'research value' for posterity. What happened with the books or other printed documents 'rejected' by both the libraries? During my ten years tenure with the British Museum Library (1959–69), I checked for some specific books that were listed in *Gazette Notifications of India* but not recorded in either of these two libraries' catalogues and hand-lists. I could not get any suitable answer from any corner. The two libraries in London retained only the books, etc., they considered 'useful'; the rest were gifted away.

The Act has undergone thirteen amendments between 1890 and 1960. However, major provisions remained unchanged, compelling the delivery of copies of each book, periodical and newspaper for the scrutiny of state government agencies

(Ramasamy, 2003). To a large extent the Press and Registration of Books Act continues to be 'active' like many such acts and regulations as part of colonial hegemony. In this specific case, the government of the day allowed it to be adopted as the provision of a 'safety net' but in reality allowed one or more 'free' copies of a book and other materials printed in the State to be acquired for a few libraries of choice, including one extra copy to be deposited in theParliament Library, New Delhi (copy was earlier sent to London). This was adopted by several States to ensure access to most local publications 'useful' to citizenry. Surely, the Parliament Library has always been in a relatively better financial position to spare extra funds to acquire every suitable Indian publication from the open market? The revised legislation may allow one copy of all EHSU language-category publications to be delivered, free of cost to the Parliament Library.

The present practice of depositing a copy or copies of books, etc., published within the state, in a few selected public libraries, in return for bringing out regularly a list/bibliography of current publications in *Gazette Notifications*, cannot be accepted as a just and fair practice. Each state would be allocating annual grants to buy multiple copies of current publications for its public library system. To acquire one or two extra copies of the books could not be considered an overwhelming extra burden on the state exchequer. To bring out the current national bibliography of Indian publications is a job assigned to the National Library/CRL, listing books received under the Delivery of Books Act (1954). *INB* should be brought out in four fascicules, regularly and promptly listing all current Indian books which could increase its utility many fold if the author and title of every book listed is added in its original script also.

According to Paul (2008), books are still received by the Registrar of Publications, West Bengal but the present condition of maintaining the said catalogues and their quarterly publications (as part of the state gazette notifications) are just chaotic and virtually non-existent. Most of the printers/publishers deposit copies of their publications once in a year. They respond only when the state government through a press insertion, invite local publishers to deposit copies of current year's publications for preparation of the annual select list of books (intended for public library purchase also). Annual bulk purchase practice for the state public libraries is the main motivating factor to deposit copies under PR Act.

He cited several research papers on the present status of bibliographic control under PR Act, for Bengali, Marathi, Telugu, Urdu and Kannada publications in India, which are not encouraging either.

However, we have to consider a separate line of action dealing with serials–periodicals and newspapers. There are multiple issues/editions of the same newspapers and periodicals, both in printed and electronic formats; some are in different languages published at regular frequencies or just brought out irregularly at the discretion of publishers/printers. The same periodical or newspaper may change its title at any time; some change their frequency, place of publication, printer, publisher, editor or even stop publishing at any point of time within its life span. The majority of newspapers and magazines, and several research journals/periodicals are also being brought out on inferior quality paper (newsprint with a high pH value) resulting in severe problems in handling and archival preservation. Many of these are currently published also in electronic format; a few academic and research journals are being brought out only in e-format. Because of these characteristics most nations have made some appropriate legal provision and identified an agency to keep track of this category of publications.

The PR Act has been amended from time to time and recently the Ministry of Information and Broadcasting, Government of India informed through a press release that the Act is again in the process of further revision. However, the act in its present conceptual format may not be feasible for application in the case of e-books, where the author/publisher has the sole right to write/rewrite/edit as and when required, and to distribute/allow access to it is the sole prerogative of the author/publisher. The Act continues to reflect the old philosophy of the state acting as an interventionist and in the changed context in the country it would continue to sustain an anachronistic image. We would suggest the new revised Act could be called only The Press Registration Act, 1867 (revised) by removing the section 'Part V: Registration of Books'. The fast-changing and innovative printing and publication technologies would surely justify this correctional step.

Copyright Act of India, 1957 (6th revision 2013)

In the UK the Copyright Act of 1911 provides that the British Library (former British Museum) shall, as of right, receive within one month after publication a copy of every book published in the United Kingdom. The origins of legal deposit, however, preceded the founding of the British Museum and its continuous operation over several hundred years has contributed very largely to the library becoming the largest general collection of British publications of all periods. According to Charles A. Goodrum and Helen W. Dalrymple (1982), In the United States there had been copyright legislation in 1790, 1846, 1859, 1865 and 1867 during which years the place of deposit was shifted from one agency to another, till the copyright law was finally passed in 1870 declaring that all records and other things related to copyrights and required by law to be preserved, shall be under the control of the Librarian of Congress and that includes anyone claiming a copyright on any book, map, chart, dramatic or musical composition, engraving, cut, print, or photograph.

There is similar legislation in several other countries that allow national libraries to receive one or more copies of all publications of that country. It would have been simpler and easier to implement, if the issue of legal deposit had been incorporated by amending the Copyright Act of India instead of introducing a separate act (DB Act) for the same purpose. Currently different concerned ministries of the centre government are active in revising all the three acts, Copyright Act, Press and Books Registration Act and Delivery of Books Act, without setting up any institutional coordination mechanism at any level. We would like to make a serious appeal to the government of India to revise the Copyright Act in conformity with many of the advanced western countries, to allow the National Library to receive one copy of every 'publication' brought out within India in every format and medium for public use and distribution.

Several issues relating to major policy issues as well as administrative and professional factors that are required to be attended to by the National Library and the concerned ministry of the Government of India. These ideas crept up over the last few decades of my direct or indirect association with the library at different points of time. Perhaps it would be appropriate for the authorities to consider setting up a high-powered committee or commission to draw up some working model of India's library systems and services to be fully operational in terms of its shape and size by 2020 where the National Library shall be on the proposed revision of the Delivery of Books Act, 1954 as we also believe with many others identified as its hub (see for example, the UK's Dainton Committee, 1969).

The limitations and consequent maladies in our library systems were caused partly by several impediments of the DB Act. The Act has been a major factor in the present stagnation in the growth of the National Library but surely not the only or even the primary one. It may look strange to realise that Indian Delivery of Books (Public Library) Act, 1954 only permits public libraries in four regions of India to receive copies of publications. I am not sure why 'public library' was specified in the act. Perhaps the National Library's origin started as a local public library (Calcutta Public Library) could possibly be the root cause. Again, the Library is still providing such services as, lending (against some amount of security deposit) and a separate children's section–the two very distinctive characteristics of a public library. Usually a national library is expected by the patrons as 'library for the last call'whereas, in Kolkata it has been providing services as 'a library of first call' to a large section of regular clientele. To allow the library to be under the administrative control of the centre government as a subordinate office, for nearly one hundred years, could be another main cause of our short-sighted policy decisions.

Perhaps it is too late to raise the original idea of shifting the Central Reference Library to have a permanent home in Delhi. I consider time is running out for us to find some appropriate location in Delhi to retain the collections of the Central Secretariat Library and National Social Science Documentation Centre Library (ICSSR); already these collections have lost thousands of volumes together with a large number of their users. The National Library could be allowed to take over these two libraries and make them part of its separate 'Lending Library Collections'. This combined collection together with its proposed ISSN and ISBN units could be moved into a suitable building in New Delhi. There is nothing uncommon about this proposal as one can look at the British Library's lending section being housed in Boston Spa, Yorkshire, while the main Library continues to be in the heart of London. Another weakness in the Indian library world is the lack of any lobbying body or pressure group, such as professional associations, that could act as an effective watch dog. The sad part of the story is that when a library and its scope were either widened or reduced (e.g., Central Secretariat Library or NASSDOC Library it has always been based on an executive decision and not otherwise. On the other hand, when a Committee or Commission was set up to review the future of any major library systems or services, such reports are mostly 'being shelved' by the concerned authorities.

References

1. Abhram, Thomas (2011), 'E-books: How Will The Digital Age Change Publishing?' *Indian Express*, 3rd November, 2011.
2. Bandopadhyay, A. R. (2000), 'Delivery Of Books Act, 1954–Suggestions For A Fresh Look', *ILA Bulletin*, 36(3), 2000, pp. 69–79.
3. *Delivery of Books Act, 1954 (amended 1956).*
4. India, Ministry of Culture (2010), *'Annual Report 2009–10'*, pp. 187-88. http://www.indiaculture.nic.in/indaculture/pdf/MoC%20Report%202009-2010.pdf (visited 22.2.12).
5. Lariviere, Jules (2000), *Guidelines of Legal Deposit Legislation.*, rev. and enlarged ed. Paris: UNESCO, 2000.
6. *Legal Deposit Libraries Act 2003,* http://www.legislation.hmso.gov.uk/acts/acts2003/20030028.htm(visited 11/10/11).
7. Lunn, Jean (1981), *Guidelines for Legal Deposit Legislation*, Paris: UNESCO, 1981.
8. Malhotra, D.N. (2010), 'Globalisation: Its Impact On Indian Publishing'. *Granthana*, 5(1), 2010, pp. 63–70.
9. Mallya, Vinutha (2011), 'The Indian Invitation: Why India Makes A Perfect Publishing partner', *Publishing perspectives*, April 19 2011. http:// publishingperspectives.com/2011/04/the- Indian-invitation-publishing/ (visited 17/08/11).
10. National Knowledge Commission (2006) *'Libraries, Gateways To Knowledge: A Road-Map For Revitalisation'* (based on the Recommendations of the Working Group on Libraries), http://www.knowledgecommission.gov.in/downloads/documents/wg_lib.pdf.(visited22.2.12).
11. National Library, Kolkata (2007). *The National Library, India: An Intellectual Resource (NACONAL 2006)*, Kolkata: National Library, 2007.

12. Paul, Dibyendu (2008). 'The Press And Registration Of Books Act And The Bibliographic Control of Bengali Publications', *Annals of Library and Information Studies*, 55(3), 2008. pp. 176-184.
13. *Press and Registration of Books Act, 1867.*
14. Ramasamy, C.R. (2003), 'National Bibliographic Control', in, Raju, A.A.N. and Ramaiah, L.S. (eds), *National Bibliographic Control: Problems And Perspectives*, New Delhi: Allied, 2003. pp. 84-92.
15. UK Department of National Heritage (1997) *Legal Deposit Of Publications: A Consultation Paper*, February 1997, London: Department of National Heritage.

4
Public Library Service – Users and Resources*

Introduction

The term "public library" is used very loosely in India. It is used to denote any library which permits the public in general, to use its services free of charge in most cases or on some nominal payment for borrowing books, magazines, videos, CDs and other items. Because of this broad interpretation of the term, the statistics published by UNESCO in 1956 show that India leads the world in having the largest number of public libraries 24,086, while UK, USA, Denmark and Sweden have only 618, 7,500, 1,329 and 3,507 public libraries, respectively.

The concept of public library emerged in India towards the end of nineteenth century along with the upheaval of nationalism. It was in the middle of twentieth century that most of the states accepted the need for library services as a vital tool for social reconstruction. Public library development is a state subject as per the Constitution of India and with more pressing claims, they found it difficult to mobilise additional resources for this purpose. However, many states and union territories have established State central libraries and libraries at the district, block and village levels.

The earliest efforts to set up public libraries had been made in the princely state of Baroda Punjab and Andhra Pradesh.

* Presented at the Seminar for Northern States on Public Library Scenario in the 21st Century, New Delhi 21-22 May 1998, RRRLF as the Keynote address. [*in GRANTHANA* 8 (1-2), 1999. 87-94] – revised

Dr Ranganathan drafted a Model Public Library Bill in 1930, and it took him almost two decades of perseverance and personal efforts for enacting the Madras Public Library Act (1948), the first of its kind in India. Today, 16 states have enacted public library legislation but in a few, Act is yet to be fully implemented.

Actual number of public libraries in India is yet to be ascertained due to lack of required statistical data collection efforts at several levels. Raja Rammohun Roy Library Foundation (RRRLF) under the Ministry of Culture, Government of India has undertaken a project to compile *Directory of Indian Libraries*, an online database. When this will be available for public use is anybody's guess. However, if we include the privately run libraries (registered under the Societies Registration Act of 1860) their number may exceed 75,000 within the 29 states and the union territories of India. Role of the centre government is largely promotional for public libraries in general is usually channeled through the RRRLF which was established in 1972 by the centre government to promote and support the public library movement and develop reading habits among the people.

During the Seventh Five Year Plan (1985-1990), the entire library and information scenario in the country was reviewed and a National Policy for Library and Information Systems was formulated (1986) for the first time. Same year a new education policy and a separate book policy documents were also prepared and made available in the public domain. Unfortunately, all these documents did not give much weightage on public library development issues.

Library Service

Public libraries have an important role in supplementing the formal educational system and of providing a local centre for life-long continuing education according to the needs and convenience of individuals. In a country where nearly half of the population cannot read and write, public libraries can help in spreading literacy and preventing people from lapsing back into illiteracy. A library makes a substantial contribution in socio-economic and cultural developments in every social milieu. It provides access to information, extends support in leisure reading and helps to open up opportunities for personal creative developments.

The revised *UNESCO Public Library Manifesto, 1994* considers 'the public library as a living force for education, culture and information, and an essential agent for the fostering of peace and spiritual welfare through the minds of men and women'. The *Manifesto* lists 12 missions that should form the core services of a public library. These revised missions have taken note of the life styles of individuals and different communities in today's world. Moreover, this revision stresses the need for the public library to play a major role in bringing art and culture, games and sports on the centre-stage together with literacy and life-long education. RRRLF and other Indian public and private sector organisations that are directly or indirectly associated with library development issues, must take note of this factor.

Every library designs its services based on four of its main components: (1) users, (2) resources, (3) library staff and (4) physical amenities. Users' community is pivotal to all library activities—its nature and composition in terms of age, sex, literacy, education, socio-cultural background and life-style. Living environment, economic constraints and non-availability of suitable reading materials at the right time are also some major factors that affect the pattern of library use. With high percentage of illiteracy and low level of education combined with language barriers are the major parameters that would have direct impact on reading habits of individuals and their numbers, in every part of India. A large number of educated users are the first generation school and college goers from their respective families. A book as a living companion is not commonly accepted by large majority of Indian households. Reading for pleasure, a pastime, is yet to be inculcated among Indians at large. Individual book buyers, for his or her private collection has been an uncommon phenomenon. However, with the growth of per capita income this trend is positively moving higher over the last two decades. Book as a 'gift' item is still limited to a small section of our population. A large section of our young professionals usually limit their reading habits to newspapers, magazine and light fictions once they join the professional workforce. These days a large part of their time is spent in reading anything and everything on software format on computer monitors. I know a few who got *Amazon Kindle* or *e-Reader Touch* for any leisure reading.

Reading material in all the public libraries basically comprises of printed books, magazines and newspapers. A large majority of these are in the languages read and spoken by the local people, including English. Nearly 50 per cent of the annual Indian language publications can be grouped under literature and another 15-20 per cent will be school text books and some meant for undergraduate studies. The remaining 30 per cent or so may include reference books, social sciences and other non-fiction categories, including religion and philosophy. According to a recent survey conducted by NBT, about 6-18 per cent of these could be put as children literature. Books in Hindi, English, Bengali and Malayalam are proportionately more numerous in topics.

Most of the Indian public libraries – irrespective of their location, urban or rural – are not being used to its full potential. One of the main reasons is lack of enough choice of suitable reading material. Libraries are having few non-book materials, such as, audio, video tapes and cassettes, computer with internet accessibility, photographs, posters, paintings, live shows, lectures, movies, etc. A few other reasons could be grouped together, e.g., easy access to a close-by cafeteria for tea, coffee or snacks, depressing interior, seating arrangements are not relaxing enough, etc. Take for example the wide range of facilities that are now available in several public libraries in the west were unthinkable even before 2000 AD. To put it in short, a local library must be an integral part of the community's day to day life and proactive in every sector of services offered.

Audio-visual material for public libraries constitutes a major component of its resources. Its availability, collection and development need careful judgement by the library management. In addition, the digital technology together with the fast growing e-book publication, have opened up a vast sector of information resources for every type of library. This new technological innovation has already brought in a completely new perception in library management where a reader may have direct online access to metadata and all textual library resources on electronic format, irrespective of its location, without visiting a library. RRRLF has recently started providing some support to public libraries with TV sets and computers inclusive of regular training facilities to library staff. This has helped in modernisation of several public library services including increase in the number of library visitors.

What is known as extension service in a public library should be considered as part of the whole, compared to stocking of only large number of printed reading materials in Indian context where the total figure of illiteracy is very high. This positive change in public libraries has improved the number of daily visitors who spend a good amount of leisure hours for entertainment, recreational or social exchange of issues relevant to their daily life. Naturally, this would also generate more demand for information and improve reading habits.

Quality of book production in India has considerably improved over the last few decades, the main weakness of Indian book trade is–marketing and distribution–continues to be overwhelming. As a result, print order of an English new title is comparatively less (300-500 copies for research monographs) which naturally implies higher pricing. However, with the recent trends of economic growth there is noticeable improvement in this sphere as well during the last two decades.

Library Acquisition

Fund allocation for the purchase of book and other reading materials has always been relatively low in all worldwide public libraries. But this is more acute in general in a developing country like India. A large portion of it is usually spent on acquiring light reading material, magazines and newspapers. Public libraries funded by the state governments have a centralised procurement policy for both annual acquisition of reading materials and all other items required/consumed by libraries. In a few states, more than one copy of every title published within the respective state, are acquired under the Press and Registration of Books Act 1867 which to my mind is morally an unhealthy practice on the part of the state. Bulk purchase of such reading material are being done on the basis of open tender, for all other branch libraries located at district headquarters or at various rural locations. This Act is under consideration of some revision by the central government. The draft revised version excludes this particular provision of the Act.

Other than providing matching grants to State Public Library authorities, RRRLF also donates books direct to several district public libraries. With the passage of time and the impact of information and communication technologies, there is a strong and urgent need to procure non-book materials (audio-visual, Braille, *e*-publications) for these libraries. By acquiring only print materials, we are actually depriving our young readers in a big way. This issue was being brought up long back, time and again, by me as a member of the foundation. It was also proposed that the RRRLF could produce and distribute some audio-visual materials on topics, such as, 'how to use a library', 'a day in a public library', etc. I was not successful during my days except in arranging to provide a few TV sets only but I gather, RRRLF has recently changed its policy in favour of audio visual material.

Bibliographic Control Of Indian Publications

A large majority of Indian public libraries process (cataloguing and classification) each book separately by their own staff, whereas all books are being centrally acquired by their respective state central library. It is difficult to understand why this colossal wastage of costly professional manpower is made by undertaking so much of repetitive work at every library unit or branch library. There has been much positive development in Indian library system and services during the last fifty odd years, since independence, but this is one sector where we have failed miserably indeed.

If only the National Library and or the Central Reference Library, Kolkata would have taken full responsibilities of delivering this particular service by organising a time bound smooth distribution system of records (e.g., catalogue cards) prepared for each book received by it from Indian publishers under the Delivery of Books Act, then Indian librarianship would perhaps have taken a different course of growth. It would have been a different story if the *Indian National Bibliography* had been up-to-date with Central Reference Library's one-time venture of card catalogue distribution being sustained. It is a fact that about 80 per cent (if not more) of the annual intake of an Indian public library is of Indian origin. However, this figure would naturally will go downwards to about 30-40 per cent (60-70 per cent are foreign publications) when we compare this with similar annual acquisition figures of university or some specialised research institution library. It would be easy to find a scapegoat like, bureaucratic red tape, financial constraints, limited technical knowledge, or publishers' apathy towards sharing the burden, etc. But, to my mind, the major responsibility of its failure lays squarely on the Indian library profession for not having any positive foresight. Take the case of

DK Book Service (and a few other Indian book distributers) which is providing similar services for recent Indian publications, to overseas libraries on some extra payment. DKs are supplying Indian publications with soft copies of full catalogue (MARK.2) records, irrespective of language or script.

It is not always true that bibliographic control of a country is to be centralised only in the National Library. It may be undertaken by bodies, such as, Federation of Indian Publishers (FIP), Federations of Indian Booksellers and Publishers Associations (FIBPA) or some private agency take up this assignment purely as a commercial enterprise. We all are familiar with the monthly publication *South Asia Accession List*, started in early 1960s, brought out by the US Library of Congress Office, New Delhi, based on its acquisition programme of Indian publications. It was used as a check list for current Indian publications by many Indian academic and foreign libraries in the absence of a current and comprehensive *Indian National Bibliography*. The Library of Congress stopped this publication in early 1990s with the introduction of computer and internet access in more and more libraries. Like *INB*, the *Accession list* of the LC also was having a limited use to Indian public libraries. There has been a long demand by Indian publishers and library organisations to revise the Delivery of Books Act, 1954 that allowed four regional libraries, including the National Library, Kolkata to receive a copy of all Indian publications available on sale. This Act reached the stage of obsolescence long back. It is in the process of revision at the government, India, level for over a decade now. Several shortcomings of the Act are the main reasons the National Library is facing continuous hardship in making the *INB* a comprehensive current national bibliography.

During early 1980s, application of computers for housekeeping operations was initiated in Indian libraries. But it is only in the 90s that librarians have realised how essential a computer is in every sphere of library activities. To meet the specialised manpower requirement a massive training programme was introduced both at the BLISc level and short term specialised in service training facilities for the working library staff which were being carried out at various levels within India, largely sponsored by GoI through its NISSAT project under the Department of Scientific and Industrial Research and University Grants Commission and several other local professional organisations. Today, we are having several indigenous software packages for library applications. We are also having a simple procedure to bring out catalogue entries in the original script as suitable software packages are being developed to meet this demand. With the availability of advanced communication technologies, a catalogue record produced for a Tamil book in Chennai would be just enough to supply or to allow access to this metadata or even the actual text in digital format to a library or an individual, located at any part of the country. Future library would not be a store house of information resources together with some aides prepared by librarian to allow physical access to users as and when they wish to consult them. Role of the library shall change to act more as an information hub, allowing selective access to different databases to its patrons, irrespective of the actual location or format. We know more than 50 per cent of new publications, like, books or other information sources, are being published or digitally re-formatted which could be accessed online through the internet.

The new National Mission for Libraries (NML) must recommend for the RRRLF and organisations like the National Library to join hands for bringing in Indian library services to get merged as equal partners of this dynamic global library services. Time has already run out. Indian publishers, professional library organisations and other stakeholders should jointly find out a solution to this critical issue at the earliest.

If we become successful in bringing out an online current bibliography of Indian publications as language fascicules in their respective scripts, 50 per cent of the problems directly related to qualified manpower issues faced by our library systems would no doubt be solved in no time. This factor has kept a large section of qualified library staff bogged down to repetitive jobs which could be avoided by introducing centralised processing of books and other documents procured by the State public library systems. This would also help in reviewing the BLISc curriculum of all library science schools of the country which is presently producing a massive number of half-baked professionals; a large number of these get lost in the wilderness.

Education And Training In Library And Information Science

The issue of Library and Information Science (LIS) manpower development is directly affecting public library development. There are about 200 departments of library and information science attached to several Indian universities that are conducting full time courses, to bring out over 15,000 to 20,000 BLISc (about 80 per cent of the total), MLISc, M.Phil and Ph.D. post-graduate degree holders every year. Indira Gandhi National Open University (IGNOU) and several other universities are also running similar courses in library and information science fields through correspondence only. Many of the state library associations and several polytechnics are also running diploma or certificate courses in library and information field. Curriculum and syllabi of most of these organisations are largely oriented towards academic libraries' manpower requirements. In addition, we are having NISCARE (earlier INSDOC) and DRTC running a two years full-time post-graduate specialisation course to cater to the special needs of R and D institutions. Many of these organisations started these courses during 1960s to meet a heavy demand of library professionals due to rapid growth in number of new schools, colleges and other educational institutions all throughout the country. It is evident from the above facts that not much attention was given towards the need of public libraries while designing the curriculum. Due to slow down of economic growth of India since 1990s, it has some impact on every sphere of human activities including the educational institutions. It is significant to note that this economic slowing down did have little impact on the number of new library schools and their annual turn out of fresh librarians. Earlier the entire curriculum and syllabi are heavily tilted towards cataloguing and classification (60 per cent of time in training and course work); application of computer in libraries is only a recent addition to the course content. Public library staff is required to have some special knowledge to deal with community development programme, e.g. environment, health and hygiene, agriculture, adult education, entertainment, etc., handling of A.V. material, skill in communication through display and other promotional activities to make the library to be one of the major community participating centres through various daily extension activities. Things may improve if some experienced and successful senior public library management experts are also associated with the staff training programmes conducted by these library science schools. It is not that 'public library' is not covered within the course content. But most of it is theoretical based on foreign publications and experience. Education in library science has got to be modernised fast. Knowledge of 'application of computer in libraries' can never be considered adequate enough as a skill for future library management. We shall continue to live with our present mediocrity if special attention is not been given on public library services urgently in designing our course curriculum

The best of the lot of qualified professionals from these schools prefer to get jobs in universities or some research organisations. Of the rest, a small percentage may end up in finding their way for a job in a public library or a school library as the last choice. However, a large percentage of them remain unemployed or under employed for several years together. Secondly, their number is too large for them to find suitable placements unless the demand grows with high infrastructural development in all sectors of national economy. Thirdly, we must introduce some specialisation within the LIS training curriculum suitable for public library service that will surely bring some positive visible changes in our public library systems. Till now it is running as a poor third as compared to special and academic libraries.

Impact Of Electronic Media And Information Technology

Electronic media, computer and telecom technologies are bringing in rapid changes in our social, educational, entertainment and every segment of our daily social life and activities. These changes are continuously making some impact, one way or the other, on every individual, irrespective of our liking or disliking it. Younger generation with an inquisitive mind is the primary target who are ready to accept or 'ready to have a go at it' for all kinds of change. Obviously, these changes or technological innovations are taking place first (with a few exceptions) in the developed countries. In Indian library domain, we guess, there is a big gap of about two decades, in the application of these technological innovations which is a serious concern for all of us to get the full benefit in terms of access and services offered by the libraries. It may sound though pessimistic but we must accept-a race or process of being compatible enough-it may be very difficult but not impossible to catch up with the gap thus created, due to several coherent factors including lack of R and D activities in library management. No doubt, it also requires a large capital investment for building up infrastructure and redesigning the manpower development programmes. We must also accept it takes time to bring in effective changes at the operational level.

Some changes or library modernisation, with the help of new technologies have been introduced effectively in several libraries attached to research organisations (especially in science and technology fields) and in a few universities. A few state public library systems have recently brought in machine readable catalogues including few other house-keeping applications at district and main branch libraries. All the catalogues of different libraries shall have to be inter-linked on their respective web sites is a task which must be taken up by the profession and library authorities. These technologies are now available in India. DELNET type of network services, that are actually based on union catalogue concept shall become obsolete with the introduction of more and more e-publications and coordinated universal access to digitisation projects. Let us not forget that our first task is to make the library services real effective by adopting well-established standards through conventional methods and by setting up a centralised body that shall be responsible to design and control the national digital library network, including reformatting of select print resources on some cooperative guidelines applicable to all participating libraries of India. We know computers just cannot bring in all the expected positive changes in our libraries. However, we are not yet aware of the transformations that will be brought in soon in library services, through Internet and a small hand set gadget like, mobile phone, tablets, we all are so familiar with, that are continuously bringing in 'changes' in our everyday life.

The whole concept of library and information service which is in practice now – based on predominantly print media, shall have to be multimedia inclusive with the advent of more and more integrated approach of advanced information and communication technologies. In terms of library service modernisation, what many of us have experienced during the last fifty years, the next fifty years shall bring in more rapid changes with wider choice on a big platter at a speed that is surely at this stage, beyond imagination.

5

Raja Rammohun Roy Library Foundation (RRRLF) – Future Role

At the time of India's independence (1947), there were about 1,000 public libraries[1] (*Sinha Committee Report,* 1959). These were mostly subscription libraries, which means, any one wishes to borrow books shall pay monthly/annual subscription to avail such facilities under several rigid rules and regulations. Many of these, however, allowed free reading room services to the local community (books, newspaper, magazine, etc.). The Report indicated poor state of affairs, "stagnant pools of books" in some dark non-descriptive locations. The condition of many of these old public libraries in rural and urban set up have not changed much over the last few decades due to genuine financial problems. Some of these libraries, I have visited during the last two decades, are keeping the doors opened much because of the grants received from the Raja Rammohan Roy Library Foundation.

Recently, I had a chance to look at the RRRLF *40th Annual Report*[2] *(2011-12)* which reminded me of the exactly similar type of reports brought out by the foundation, both in format and content during the eighties, when I was a member of the foundation for a few years. Earlier it used to be brought out in mimeographed rather than a computer print out. Noticeable difference is the increase in number of libraries served and also the increase in number of schemes for allocation of grants provided now to organisations and state government agencies. The latest *Report* does not indicate the total number of libraries received assistance during 2011-12 from the foundation.

RRRLF is an 'autonomous' organisation established in 1972 with full financial allocation from the central government (Ministry of Culture) with sole objective of providing back up support to all states and union territories (UTs) in taking library services to every corner of the country. One must consider this as a significant move by the central government, in the light of the fact that 'library' is a matter to be dealt by state governments according to the Constitution of India. By 1972, when the foundation was born, there were only four states (Tamil Nadu, 1948; Andhra Pradesh, 1960; Karnataka, 1965 and Maharashtra, 1967) having adopted their own separate library legislations. One must not also miss the point recorded in this *Annual Report* of the foundation that out of the 35 States and UTs, the twenty eight (28) that have adopted library legislation are providing better and wider library service network as compared to others.

Since inception the foundation is functioning as a donor, distributing funds to state and UT governments to buy books and other reading resource materials for their public libraries and also supplying new publications and other items direct to libraries for the benefit of the users. During 2011-12, the foundation gave away grants over Rs 358 million and spent about 11.33 million rupees gross, roughly four per cent of the grant amount on administrative overhead. The foundation also claims to function 'as a national agency for coordinating, monitoring and developing public library service in the country.

Annual administrative expenses incurred by the foundation to act as a donor agency, compared to its budgetary allocation may be considered as reasonable. What puzzles me is the small amount spent on other sectors which Foundation claimed to be a 'national agency' for coordination, monitoring and developing public library service in the country. Take the following schemes: (i) Assistance towards collection and compilation of library statistics through official and non-official agencies; (ii) Assistance to libraries for celebration of golden jubilee, centenary, etc. and

(iii) Assistance to libraries/organisations to organise seminar, training, conferences, etc. No amount was spent under item (i) and 91 million rupees was spent under (ii), (iii) and (v – Computer and A.V. materials) schemes. However over the years, foundation must have collected a large amount of data on various facets of library activities and services. Prime reason of collection, analysis of these statistical data would expect to help the management to formulate its future policy and planning strategies. However, foundation may not create much impact as libraries are governed under the rules and regulations formulated separately by different states and union territories.

Over the last four decades, RRRLF is primarily helping libraries to build up larger resource materials for reading public. We all appreciate and recognise its contribution towards the growth of public library systems and their services to our civil society. It has improved considerably but not up to the expected level of what is available in many of the western and south east Asian countries. There may be dozens of reasons for this gap between the reality and our expectations. Some of the genuine reasons applicable to India may be limited fund, illiteracy, lack of adequate transportation and communication, low education level, shortage of quality reading material in vernacular languages, television, short library hours, etc. No nationwide detail study has been conducted so far to get some conclusive results.

Foundation distributed grants during 2011–2012 to the libraries to the tune of Rs 358 million. This may increase over 500 million/year or more, in a few years, and continue to increase further with time. If we carefully evaluate this figure, we find this amount is only a tiny drop of the union government's annual budgetary allocation of funds to the state and UTs, under different heads. We must also accept the fact that the combined gross amount spent annually by the states and UT governments for public library services would exceed manifold than the amount RRRLF disburse as grants for the same cause.

There is no denying the fact that the amount allocated by the state governments for public libraries is simply inadequate. One would wonder why then this small amount for public library development was not directly allocated to state governments.

We must, however, remember the condition of public libraries in the 1970s was, in terms of figures, not so exciting. As a follow up to *Sinha Committee recommendations* (1959), Government of India started contributing to the library funds of the states equivalent to the amount of cess collected. But it was found to be utilised more to cover administrative overhead costs than to build up collections of extra reading materials. Part of the credit for this improvement in both quality and quantity must go to the foundation. One factor that may have worked to bring this new supportive service under the financial and executive control of the central government, by having a new registered society for public library development thereby avoiding the complicated legal and legislative process to amend the constitution for bringing 'library' under the concurrent list. Secondly, there has been a trend or a mind set of our bureaucratic machinery to keep all programmes and projects that require additional financial allocation that would be having some all India implications, such activities would be justified to be kept under central government control. Since 1990, however, there are some signs of not to pursue this trend any longer.

Where do we go from here? We cannot expect the foundation to continue to operate over another four/five decades, in the twenty first century, within the existing policy framework of linear growth process, to upgrade and modernise our entire public library network. It would be more appropriate for RRRLF to be functioning more and more as the national coordinating, monitoring agency for the overall growth and development of library and information systems and services of the country. As recommended by the National Knowledge Commission[3] (NKC), we are soon going to have a National Mission for libraries (NML).

Some discussion is going on to ask the foundation to coordinate the challenging task of compiling an online database of Indian libraries (NKC recommendation). There are several other sectors the foundation may shift or move over to take more responsibilities for undertaking or sponsoring survey projects to bring in essential changes in library information services and sponsor coordinated research and/conduct nationwide survey (excluding academic research) which is lacking due to shortage of fund and sponsorship. Many such activities would require direct involvement of management and marketing professional corporate organisations. For example, reading habits, use or lack of use of neighbourhood library services, cutting down the cost of preparing cataluguing and other records of books added by every library separately by introducing some online centralisation mechanism. An important activity is to prepare guide book, handbook or manual suitable in Indian conditions, to be practised in different categories of library and information systems. To bring uniformity and for data exchange, we have to have standards and specifications in every sub-fields and all house-keeping operations of library and information services and systems. To justify our services both to library users and employers, there must be some performance evaluation criteria (PEC) which are essential factors in every organisational management. Many of these may need to be constantly reviewed and/or revised after a gap of every few years.

These suggestions are not new to us. Many of them have been discussed, analysed and formally documented at different LIS forums over the last few decades. Unfortunately, there have been very little follow-up actions by the organisations and individuals in the profession. This reminds us of the 'terms and conditions' framed by the Ministry of HRD while constituting the Advisory Committee for Libraries. The first two were– (1) To enquire into the present reading needs of the people, how they are met...; and (2). To enquire into the reading tastes of various sections of the people, what agencies are there to provide suitable literature and how the reading tastes and hence the literature can be improved. As these would have led the committee into a large research projects, it confined itself to terms 3-6, that is, to investigating the present condition of library service in the country and on that basis made recommendations to the government (*Sinha Committee Report*, 1959, p.117)[4]. It is not that we cannot undertake such large scale national survey (e.g., *Census of India Reports*) but when it comes to books and libraries, there is none to foot the bill or take any initiative. Again, only recently the Working Group for Libraries of NKC has highlighted many of these sectors.

The foundation produced a *Guide for Public Libraries* in 1988 by D.R. Kalia[5] (mimeographed), which needs to thoroughly revised, and the well known document: *National Policy on Library and Information Systems; A Presentation (NAPLIS)*, 1988 by a committee constituted by Government of India[6]. However, prior to this, RRRLF appointed a committee with D.P. Chattopadhyaya as chairperson in 1981, to draft a document on the national policy on library and information services. The committee submitted a report[7] in 1982 that was used as the draft in formulating the *NAPLIS. A Directory of Public Libraries in India* compiled by B.P. Barua[8], former Director of the Foundation, was published in 1989. There are, I am sure, a few other similar publications with Foundation imprint, may have come out over the last couple of decades. Above list gives ample evidence of the foundation's experience and competence in handling research projects of pan-India relevance.

What is left with the foundation shall then become the core area of operation, that is, "the national agency for coordinating, monitoring and development of library services and systems in India." It may be appropriate to draw attention to the letter of 7th December, 2006 addressed to the Prime Minister, by the Chairman, National Knowledge Commission, submitting a list of ten recommendations for formulating strategies in the Library and Information Services (LIS) sector.

These recommendations were based on the report presented by its Working Group on Libraries (WGL) was attached as an annexure to the letter.

The first recommendation on the list is 'to set up a National Commission on Libraries (NML). To launch the process a National Mission on Libraries (NML) is to be set up immediately, for a period of three years. This would subsequently be expected to be converted into a permanent commission. This idea, we presume, came from the National Commission on Libraries and Information Science (NCLIS) of the United States of America and the *D.P. Chattopadhyaya Committee Report* on NAPLIS (1986). There is recently a strong movement in the United Kingdom to have a national libraries agency[9]. Weather we need to have a national commission on libraries is a matter of argument keeping in mind the current trends of socio-economic and technological developments that shall inevitably bring all categories of libraries closer by accepting modernisation process and share their resources to serve larger, assertive and more alert library users' groups. There are dozens of countries whose public library service is excellent, if not outstanding by any standard that are operating without any such central agency for libraries.

Ministry of Culture has taken initial steps to set up the National Mission on Libraries (NML). RRRLF is ideally suitable to act as an executive wing under NML and undertake the responsibilities in areas, such as, research and development, publications, data collection and analysis, preparation of LIS standards. To begin with, NML may consider of making the Foundation as an effective operational base and also allow it to keep a tab on the over all programme implementation processes of NML. This would also help when NML eventually becomes the National Commission on Libraries (NCL), the foundation could act as the main research wing and the monitoring agency. In many developed countries, such activities are performed by the national library authority and or jointly with national LIS professional associations in addition to the latter's primary role of acting as lobbyists to offer professional advice and act as a pressure group to get the best fiscal support for the growth and development of LIS profession. However, to create or develop such conditions in India within foreseeable future, I regret is beyond my imagination.

Foundation may take a planned programme of moving away from a donor agency to a research and monitoring agency within the time frame of NML and before the latter transforms to National Commission for Libraries. During the initial few years, foundation takes up, on priority, some research/survey projects; it simultaneously make moves to persuade the Ministry of Culture to transfer the fund for public library development direct to the state exchequers with some monitoring support from RRRLF. It is expected of the foundation to continue providing active support to some of its ongoing projects during this short transition period in addition to its new task of compiling the online database of Indian library directory which must be treated as an on going project to constantly update data and make it comprehensive. This directory shall be an essential tool for all future policy planning exercises for all types of libraries.

There is a general feeling among the librarians that users are moving away from libraries. We do not have actual figures as no such comprehensive research was being undertaken in India. As a result, we continue to follow the conventional routes on public library development and adopt a 'hope for the best' kind of attitude. Grindlays and Morris[10] published their findings on the decline in adult book lending in UK public libraries. This is a key document and should be read by anyone interested in trends in public libraries usage over the late twentieth and early twenty-first centuries. They found that the underlying causes were probably, increasing affluence making book purchase more affordable, and wide spread use of internet and home PCs. Other causes could be increasing cost of books and journals which affects lesser new books added to libraries, and inconvenient opening days/hours.

OCLC[11] published a major survey on people's perception of libraries and information services. This report covered users in North America, the UK, Australia, Singapore and India. Its methodology was limited as the research was based on internet and English language users only. There were several key messages: the library brand is the 'book'; there is a strong attachment to libraries but that attachment is based upon nostalgia; and respondents have strong attachments to the idea of the 'library' but clearly expressed dissatisfaction with the service experience of the libraries they use. Poor signage, inhospitable surroundings, unfriendly staff, lack of parking, dirt, heat/cold, hard-to-use systems and inconvenient hours were mentioned many times. The overall message was clear: improve the physical amenities and experience of using libraries.

Whenever we talk about development of public library services we find 'comprehensive, efficient and modern' are the terms prefixed to it. In Indian context, it is difficult to comprehend by LIS management and policy makers. The first time in 1998, Public Library Standards (19) were introduced in UK for reviewing their services internally. The standards had been refined[12] to 10 in 2004-05 covering: distance people travel to reach a local library static/mobile; aggregate opening hours; number of libraries with internet access; number of electronic work-stations; request-supply time; number of visits; users satisfaction; number of books purchased; length of time it would take to replenish the lending stock. Another important report[13] submitted in 2005 by the British House of Commons Culture, Media and Sports Committee, contained over thirty recommendations and in its final paragraph it puts two key recommendations: (1) libraries' fundamental role in promoting reading and seek to distinguish between core functions and desirable add-ons; and (2) need to have stronger links between national library standards and effective mechanisms to encourage and enable library services to meet, if not surpass, them. The important point is that the standards are essential requirements for any such management review of Indian public library services. Without such standards it is less likely that cultural services and library services in particular, could be taken seriously enough for Comprehensive Performance Assessment (CPA) or for any such evaluation process.

It has been agreed that British public library services are one of the best in today's world. There have been continuous review and research activities by both public and private organisations to bring public libraries as an integrated component of national information resources and delivery systems but also to make sure it continuously sustain its rightful position within the national library hub. Any serious student of librarianship will not miss the large amount of research publications produced both in public and private sectors, in the UK annually. Secondly, we must remember that Delhi Public Library was set up at the initiative of UNESCO, by Government of India, on the model of British public library services in the early sixties and the present day Indian public library network in all the states followed by and large the same UK pattern. Hence, we find it justified to focus more on recent British publications relevant to our topic of discussion.

Primary objective of the foundation is to provide support to stimulate continuous improvement in library services thereby increasing the number of library users and motivate the left-outs within every age group of a community. This would obviously mean, even by the existing traditional practices, more than just annual augmentation of annual book stock of libraries. And by modernisation we must look, beyond computerisation of house-keeping operations of libraries, to a newer set of exemplary public libraries in Britain. Idea Stores in Tower Hamlets and Discovery Centres[14] in Kent and Hampshire share similar aims and would likely to excite our imagination. These are housed in a series of bright, new buildings in local shopping areas, combining lifelong learning and cultural attractions with all the services normally associated with libraries from classic books to DVDs and CDs and internet access. A place where skills and training advice is freely available and courses are offered in the same building; a place where one can relax in a quality café, take in an art exhibition or music performance or a quiet place where one would seat for doing school homework, or allow to have fun and chat with your friends. No, one would not expect all future public libraries to be having all these in India but surely we can take a bold move of experimentation in a few, urban and semi-urban locations. There are a few libraries run by private sector organisations in Delhi may serve as a kind of model to make a beginning.

Framework for the future is a long term strategic vision for our library services. The proposals are presented as a framework to encourage imaginative and innovative and greater operational involvement at both governmental and library professional levels. It could nevertheless provide a vision of a library service in the opening decades of the twenty first century. Delivery of the vision is to be handled partly by RRRLF with a plan of action that will divide the tasks into packages by NML among the state public library authorities with specific strategic objectives. The National Knowledge Commission and its Working Group for Libraries' report may help us to make a beginning, though one would imagine these will be revised and updated as we move along towards the goal of achieving effective and efficient Indian library systems.

References

1. Ministry of HRD, India. *Report of the Advisory Committee for Libraries, 1959.*

2. Raja Rammohun Roy Library Foundation, *Annual Report,* (40th), 2011-12.
3. National Knowledge Commission, Chairman's Letter dated 7th December, 2006, addressed to the Prime Minister of India.
4. *ibid.*, p.117.
5. D.R. Kalia: *Guide For Public Libraries*, RRRLF, 1988 [mimeographed].
6. Department of Culture, *National Policy On Library And Information Systems: A Presentation Report* (Chairman: D.P.Chattopadhyaya), 1988.
7. Raja Rammohan Roy Library Foundation, *National Policy On Library And Information Services* (Report of the Committee, Chairman: D.P.Chattopadhyaya), 1982.
8. B.P. Barua, *Directory of public libraries in India*, 1989.
9. Charles Leadbeater, *Overdue: How To Create A Modern Public Library Service. A Laser Foundation Report* London, Demos, 2003.
10. Douglas J.C. Grindlays and Anne Morris, 'The Decline In Adult Book Lending In UK Public Libraries And Its Possible Causes', *Jr. of Documentation* 60(6), 2004, 609-31.
11. *Perceptions of libraries and information resources:* a report to the OCLC membership. Dublin, Ohio: OCLC, 2005.
12. Great Britain Department for Culture, Media and Sports, Libraries, Information and Archives Division, *Comprehensive, Efficient And Modern Public Libraries: Standards And Assessment.* London: 2001
13. Great Britain, House of Commons, Cultural, Media and Sport Select Committee Report, *Comprehensive, Efficient And Modern Public Libraries*, 2005.
14. '*What's the great idea?*' Idea Store website: http://www.ideastore.co.uk (accessed 26/4/09); Dover Discovery Centre: http://www.discoverycentres.co.uk (accessed 26/4/09).

6

Digital Library of India – Consortiun Approach

I sometimes feel that I am in the midst of some very exciting and challenging time to libraries and librarians and almost wish I were able to start a career all over again. I do not work in a library. I do not have easy access to subscription databases and e-journals so easily. For someone who had association with and working experience of several large libraries in and outside India, today, I feel as if I am at the driver's seat of a bullock-cart on library highways. I am looking at the fast moving and complex digital library issues just like an old library professionalhand or some information seeking Indian citizen.

Indian libraries have been dealing with digital information resource issues over the last 20 years. Librarians took the lead when they converted card catalogues into searchable databases; however, retrospective conversion is still on going in many of these libraries. Several research and higher education institutions have started adding electronic journals to their paper subscriptions, and then supplying bibliographic information followed by information literacy training of the library patrons and now converting unique holdings to digital formats so that others can have access without even visiting the library.

Libraries and librarians of India are gradually becoming active partners with the academic and research community; trying to ensure that students have the best resources at their disposal and required skills to engage them for lifelong learning.They are with the determined perpetual motive to push information at people all the time.

According to Nancy Davenport[1](2007), 'the most essential factors to explore the digital info-world is mobilisation and the other perhaps strengthening further of inherent characteristic of librarians in collaboration andcooperation. To accomplish a task as enormous as creating a national digital library, there are colleagues to consult, associations or organisational umbrellas to support the project or create a new forum to deal with this.'While the National Library, Kolkata, just independently started its digitisation project, '*Down Memory Lane*' in 1999 for archiving of rare and brittle documents published prior to 1900 is not clear. It continued to pursuethe same conventional policy and practice based on the guidelines framed by committees and commissions, constituted several decades ago. Whatever changes that are being introduced recently, such as, application of computer technology, are largely because of outside pressure. Again, why Indian Institute of Sciences, Bangalurudid not included the National Library in its Digital Library of India (DLI) project ambit that started around the same time, originally sponsored by Carnegie-Mellon University? Outcome of this project helped India to bring out multilingual textbooks in digital format. The National Library is in an ideal position to take the leadership role in developing and formulating a national policy and strategies of India's National Digital Library (NDL) services and systems. Its own digitisation of rare collections is an on-going project that required to be dovetailed with all similar activities of different libraries of India. National Knowledge Commission's Working Group on Libraries avoided for some reasons, in dealing with national library issues. Good sense prevailed when the newly constituted National Mission for Libraries (NML) asked the Director General, National Library to participate as a special invitee in their first meeting held in May 2012.

Harsha Parekh[2] (2004) in her paper at the ICDL (2004) expressed serious concern of digitisation activities in India carried in a very fragmentary way. This was the situation about nine years ago that has not changed one bit till date. She cited national digital library activities in several neighbouring countries that have developed policies, strategies and structure for applying this technology in their own national contexts to ensure inter-operability, scalability and sustainability. She argued, if digital resource development has to make some progress, it needs to be organised and contribute to a common goal. Many factors would call for a coordinated plan/system for digitisation in India'.

Libraries and librarians have continued to operate over the last century onwards to select, organise, retrieve and pass on information or knowledge to the users. These are activities not the mission of the library. Information provision is continued to be the traditional role of the library. It is this role that is being challenged in the digital environment where a large segment of it could be accessed from several outside non-conventional sources. Future librarians shall be expected to gear upso as to deliver information (and knowledge) that cannot be easily handled by another agency. To identify, select and manage information and learning resources and pay the bills shall continue to be part of his/her job description, but increasingly the information procured free/paid in e-format or downloaded from web sites goes straight from the supplier to the end user without any need to 'enter' the 'library premises'.

The library of the future will most likely be a network of knowledge systems in which people and machines collaborate, especially in libraries attached to higher academic and research institutions. Accepting this reality to be the rule of the game in near future a large sector, like the National Library and public library network shall continue to perform as 'mixed bag categories' in terms of technological innovations, for a foreseeable future in India. Question may arise if there were no such thing as libraries would we continue to support and sustain them today? This elusive objective of e-learning is understandably a long and difficult quest for reaching every individual through universally acceptable e-network is as good as a utopian phenomenon.

Let us have a look at the present day internet, computer, *Facebook*, or similar social media users' scenario in India. According to a study of Internet and Mobile Association of India (IMAI)[3], India was all set to have 121 million internet users by December 2011. The figure was 100 million in September 2011. Out of this 121m, 97 million are expected to be active internet users, who access once in every month. 100 million internet users figure is considered as critical landmark for the country. Census of India[4] 2011 records there are 15.54 million household (6.3 per cent of total population) who have desktop/laptop computer out of which only 7.6 per cent households (3.1 per cent of population) have computer with internet access. However, a large number of users are accessing internet through offices, cyber cafes, etc. Taking into account the wide range of mobile phone, I-pad, etc. that allow easy internet accessand the two major data providers (1) *Google Ad Planner:* 30.7m and (2) Facebook (Largest player): 45.82 million are active internet users per month in India. To turn to libraries in this dynamic technological era, we must remember that CERN (Organisation Europ 'eennepour la Recherche Nucl 'eaire, Geneva) made an attempt about twenty years ago to find Higgs Boson effect that created a spin-off called the World Wide Web. This in turn set in motion the big, slow, radical transformation of libraries and its composite particle–the book.

E-book is now available in market for about thirty years, and is continuously on a fast track transformation process. Today, e-book is accepted as one of the primary format categories of library resources and is accepted to be a household name for a large section of western world's reading community. A large section of our younger generation figure runs into a few millions, is well versed with its application and utilities.

Web 2.0 is transforming the library in every possible way– its spaces, DNA, books and journals. Changes are noticeablein application mode of access to these resources, identification and in use. It is changing the fabric of every type of library and their physical shape; significantly establishing its designed positionin the larger social context. Training, teaching and guidance to library use and handling of learning resources are all being in the process of transformation. A variety of *Web 2.0* tools are common and, importantly applied two-ways for interaction with the library and users with feedback, and user to user. In addition, Web 2.0 applications have, in a relatively short time-span, received an enormous amount of attention from libraries, archives, museums and similar organisations. The benefits of Web 2.0 are now widely acknowledged. *Wikipedia* (popularity cannot be disputed), *Facebook, Blog, Twitter* of Web 2.0 can help in widening library's impact on its clientele[5]. Let us also keep in mind a new and emerging technology, Cloud computing that has generated much interest in library applications. It is expected that by 2020 individual library systems and services will be drawn into the Cloud. Cloud computing will also enable libraries to collaborate on the Web.

It will be possible soon for *e*-book to allow readers to annotate, comment and interact with the book and the author. *E*-book is predicted to be a joy to read and use online and highly recommended as a version of what the future 'networked book' can be. According to some experts, e-book will continue to be, at least for the foreseeable future asimple digital replication of text. Currently, we are only getting an image or replica of the typed/printed text!

In an *e*-book library where we can search through the texts of thousands phrases, words, concepts and ideas and construct 'our own text'. According to Parkes[6] (2010), 'technology is now available, with algorithm, for us to get connected and linked up with, in terms of searching. One can search with speed and precisions, in quantity and on demand, and in most cases the result is impressive. It is powerful and a feasible option but a real drudgery for any reader considering the fact that some books may be available on certain platforms or in different browsers. One has to open each e-book separately check, mark, add notes then close it before opening another *e*-book; the process goes on'. It has so much of promises, but is very tiring and a bore. One specific reason of this genuine technical drawback is due to several different proprietary software and electrical or electronic devices available to read *e*-books. How simple and advantageous a job for user would have been if he could move from a journal citation to an *e*-book chapter and back again with minimum of fuss.

There is now a proliferation of *e*-book readers available. They can provide hundreds of titles in one portable, lightweight tablet device. These devices allow readers to change in a flick the font size and page rendering. In other words, everything a print copy can offer. Looking at the current trends it is possible thatsales of digital content will eventually outstrip sales of traditional books (in major European languages, including English). A survey from the Frankfurt Book fair in 2008 indicates that this will happen within next ten years[7] (Jones, 2008). Possibly *e*-news devices will be more in demand than for *e*-book as *Orange* (in France) has rolled out a paperless newspaper on a touch-screen device, called 'Read and go' that offers updates from five major newspapers. According to Carlson[8] (2009) in *Business Insider*, it would cost the *New York Times* about twice as much the cost of providing each of its subscribers with a new *Amazon Kindle* instead. Printing the NYT shall cost twice as much as sending every subscriber a free Kindle.

Apple has the iPhone and the iPod touch – these devices are already proving to be the most popular *e*-book reader available. With the free download of Stanza, one can easily read, resise, rotate and turn a page by flicking finger on the screen and download books over the web. One can now also get Kindle books on the device. Microsoft, *Google*, Samsung and others in the trade, are all bringing out similar devices to have a share of the bigpie.

There is a plethora of schemes and plans involving mobile phone in reading books of ones'choice. Penguin, Bloomsbury and several other British publishers are planning to deliver first chapter of a novel free to mobile phone owners. Website *DailyLit*[9] will send short customised entire book in instalments by *e*-mail to blackberry, iPhone or PC. In Japan, '*keitai*'- a novel for the mobile phone users–is a phenomenon. Vodafone has launched a service bringing books to mobile phones in audio and text, and *Google* Book Search now provides mobile editions.

In the USA, Simon and Schuster, and Random House have teamed up with *Scribd*[10], a document-sharing website to provide excerpts and full texts. Taylor and Francis allow users to 'rent' access to an *e*-book for a daytosix months. Oxford Scholarship Online gives institutions subscription access to a fully searchable collection of 2,000 OUP monographs. In 2009, Bloomsbury launched a set of e-books available as free downloads. Similar *e*-publishing with accessibility is gradually becoming a common phenomenon for a large number of publishing houses in Europe, USA, Australia and Japan.

Google Books, the infinite library – the big *e*-book news is to be the *Google* agreement with the book industry. '*Google* now has 20,000 publishers in its book-scan programme. This controversial agreement means that users will soon be able to search and buy millions of titles, many of which were out of print and previously unobtainable. The scheme will be targeted at universities but will allow anyone to download any of the over seven million books already scanned by *Google*. However, *Google* estimates, it will not be an infinite library as yet and it won't manage to index all of the world's information till twenty fourth century[11].

It has now been broadly accepted that active involvement, especially for students of higher education, helps learning online use of *e*-books or networked books. This is true particularly in the form of online social network learning engagements. Some librarians may feel themselves gradually pushed into a corner by commercial moguls such as, *Google* and *Amazon*. This situation is particularly reflected within digitisation programme of the cultural heritage sector. In an editorial comment in the *Indian Express*[12] 'as part of its quest to organise the world's information and make it universally accessible and useful *Google* in concert with the Antiquities Authority of Israel is putting the Dead Sea scrolls online'. The British Library has its own on-going project of digitisation of all its south Asian manuscripts on high priority.

In 2004, National Library of Scotland[13] Edinburgh (NLS) published a new five year strategy, B*reaking Through The Walls*. It placed particular emphasis on widening access, reaching new customers, and contributing to the Scottish social inclusion agenda. This was a significant repositioning, as the library had previously regarded itself as 'library of last resort' and had actively encouraged prospective customers to look elsewhere to satisfy information requests. NLS continues to regard its preservation role as crucial but not necessarily at the expense of access any longer. Under the revised UK Legal Deposit Libraries Act, 2003 that allowed inclusion of non-print materials to be received by all repository libraries, it was felt necessary to plan for the collection and preservation on much larger quantities of 'born digital publications'.

The most important purpose of introducing digitisation in a national library shall continue to follow basic principles of library service: user needs, accessibility and usability over and above all preservation of national heritage both in print and electronic media. The library would be expected to undertake market research to ensure developments were based upon users' demands and needs (including potential users). One must keep in mind currently available printed materials on the shelves, will only permit the digitisation of a fraction of future requirements. In other words it is important to realise that this work (digital library) is prioritised with as much of an understanding of the market as possible. Hence, deciding on the size and composition of survey population shall be considered a crucial factor as the future users shall not necessarily be confined within the four walls of national library any longer. On the other hand, there shall be a sizable number of readers who would demand 24×7 online services from within and outside the country. In addition to the regular users/visitors of the library, interview data from other stakeholders, cultural organisations, libraries and academics are to be taken into account while deciding on population samples.

We all know similar policy modifications are being adopted by many national libraries duringthe last two decades. There has to be a national coordinating body with the head of national library as chairperson for guiding policy and funding issues, mass digitisation programme and other ways to develop national digital collection through a joint mandatory participatory process.

The primary objective of creating a national digital library is to save the time of existing and potential customers, allowing widest choice and access to resources (including multimedia) which would focus on both physical access to buildings and services, and remote access via the internet. The first major coordinated initiative in India was taken at the Indian Institute of Sciences, Bangalore in 2001, originally known as the Digital Library of India (DLI) project with the participation of 25 libraries but excluding the National Library. Now, this project is known as *Digital Library Initiative,* in collaboration with C-DAC[14]. The latest policy move on this matter is a recommendation adopted at its first meeting of the recently constituted National Mission for Libraries[15] on 18th May, 2012. One of its member mentioned that 180 million pages (4,40,000 books) digitised, are available on the Web and suggested NML could supplement in setting up the National Virtual Library by creating new contents. One of the four working groups constituted by NML, shall deal with this and library relevant ICT issues.

National Library[16] is also having a digitisation project that claimed to have digitised 3,20,000 pages (9,140 selected books have been scanned). Within a few years, potential library customers will be able to register for access via its websites. In terms of its digital contents, the National Library must be committed to the widest possible free access. There has to be an understanding and acceptance that knowledge and cultural resources relevant to India in particular, should be available to all citizenry. Naturally, there would be a need of legislative initiative of amending the National Library Acts, providing the delivery and entitlements with expectation of certain restrictions and control, e.g., for access to licensed online contents. This website of the National Library must sooner than later conform to international standards for allowing access to visually handicapped potential users. One must also keep in mind, while developing web content, the overwhelming popularity of common search engines for web-based information arena. However, the foremost requirement for developing such interface to the in-house textual (multimedia inclusive) digital database is to have a comprehensive metadata for all its digital objects (and printed resources on the shelves) on some common format, such as, *Word.*

It is imperative National Library would not plan in a vacuum or independently for building up a comprehensive national database of digital information resources of such magnitude. It needs to be conceptualised of a 'distributed' national digital library. As per NML resolutions of creating a National Virtual Library or National Digital Library (NVL/NDL), the concerned Working Group must take into account current digitisation programme, and availability of the largest holdings of Indian and India related printed resources at the National Library. A crucial benefit of the internet is its ability to unify collections virtually through the use of metadata and other related acceptable uniform/standardised information and communication technologies (ICT). It is increasingly preferred to accept a loosely coordinated collaborative network approach for all such institutional repository infrastructure over physical unification focusing on interoperability and partnership at the national level. To begin with it may be metadata access and exchange facilities of institutional digital collections, centralised cataloguing of specific types of material or subjects, multimedia formats, etc. One would naturally expect the NML Working Group to recommend the National Library to act as the Coordinator of the NVL/NDL of India.

The National Library should in turn take the following measures: (a) There has to be new legislation to bring an amendment to the National Library Act (including the DB Act 1954)—organisational changes; securing sufficient funding to provide simultaneously both manualand automated services; staff and organisational structures also needed to be addressed to meet new users' demands and needs, through changing skills, training and institutional and operational hierarchies; (b) preservation of print and non-print publications especially preservation of digital/*e*-publications; (c) library must consistently keep the supporting technicalstaff alert to take developmental requirements in terms of ICT; (d) users will increasingly demand accessing library systems on a 24×7 basis which will no doubt be a challenging activity and (e) engaging other professions in this complex task–shall provide significant dividends which would justify the costs. Here is an opportunity for us to rethink professional education, where we have placed obstacles in the path of change and how we define a librarian. We need to create more points of entry into the profession while dealing with the National Library taking the lead role of developing the national digital library of India.

To ensure growth on this track, it must focus on meeting a few core strategic priorities, Market research is one essential activity for the Library that would help to strike a balance between innovation and core service growth, and between appealing to the widest possible audience and developing some niche services for a few targetted groups. The Library has the limitation of conducting a nation-wide market research based on its current user population which is heavily Kolkata or at the most eastern India based. If we accept the prime mission for Indian library systems and services is to meet the widest section of users' needs then it would be logical for us to accept the library to perform as the coordinating hub of the system. It must also be accepted that by shifting towards the goal of building the National Digital Library, (not by choice alone!) the Library would certainly bring itself into the centre stage of meeting the needs of India'sbillion library users. In this new revised role, it must realise that the primary objective of all activities has to be the development of local library service as the main strategy so that local library shall be the primary gateway for the services of the end-users.

The changing process of info environment probably would take the same trends as identified elsewhere, essential for operating within digital environment and the changed user-behaviour it has caused. These changes would obviously have some impact on job descriptions of a section of its professional and management levelstaff. Library's own collections would only constitute a small part of the relevant supply of info and it faces increased competition from new sources of information. This would result perhaps increased risk of "library bypass". For a section of users, it is no longer necessary to visit a specific library in order to get the informationhe wants. This essentially required some developmental changing process which again has been on the cards of many libraries over the last two decades or so. In addition, several national and international conferences, seminars and workshops, (without even conceiving an idea of undertaking anycomprehensive national user survey) were being held during this periodto discuss in particular, the dynamics of digital library serviceswhichindicates general awareness of the problemby all librarians. There are however, several behavioural studies confined to individual organisations and citation data analysis on specific research areas that would not reflect current status of the problem of increasingly loosing traditional bondage between library and users.

An interesting overview of these tendencies of the users was reported in an OCLC's (2003) Pattern Recognition Scan[17] which emphasises on the term 'infosphere' that defined as the network of information surrounding the individual. Its general recommendation was that library services should be brought to the user's "infosphere" thus avoiding 'library bypass'. Another interesting recommendation was that libraries should invest more resources in developing and offering collaborative technologiesto users. The most common termfor this development is *Web 2.0* and its distributed collaborative applications. This would naturally imply that users would demand facilities for communication with other users and tools for further processing of info for communicating the results. This trend implies that link collections are redundant and that libraries should not try to select and present only those info resources that are best suited for the user. It would be possible for a library with its physical information collections, backed up with self-service widespread introduction to available technological devices for possible social interactions and popular commercial search engines, around the information resources. From earliest to this day, library changed or transformed over the ages by accepting and adopting requisite technological innovations from time to time. This year, *e*-mail (1972) is 40 years old and it is part of libraries both for management as well as used for information transfer activities.

Nevertheless, it still seems relevant to ask whether we need a particular institution to select, organise, retrieve, and transmit information when the Internet and search engines are in the developing process, as they are now. We would argue that there is indeed a need for such institution but that libraries generally need to shift their focus and think more strategically–from particular processes and activities to a broad formulation of the library's mission.

We know the role of a library is to facilitate the creation of knowledge. This would imply the library is to play a more proactive role than providing just information. It is avery ambitious role in a digital environment where future course is so uncertain. In order to retain and develop its traditional roleof information provision, the library services must be present in user's infosphere which means that libraries must either develop services that are sufficiently visible and effective to attract users or they must make the library's info-resources available via the user's preferred commercial search engine. Role of library services needs to be shifted from 'what is available in the library, to provide access to all what the user needs'.

It is possible, to outsource selection, acquisition and processing of materials to vendors, like so many libraries in the West, including the US Library of Congress and the British Library, London; cataloguing of materials can be shared on a national level or outsourced; handling negotiation and administration of electronic subscriptions and licenses out sourced to vendors or to another institution.

Digital libraries are to focus not only on the task of info provision but more importantly to justify the library's existence. In every possible way the library must be 'visible to the end user'. *Google* and *Amazon* have introduced a new standard for digital information provision that has increased libraries motivation to cooperate in more areas. Libraries have now realised that they have neither the skills nor the resources to deliver the functionality that users have come to expect from *Amazon* and *Google*–unless they cooperate.

Libraries have realised that users expect to get access to all available information on one or the other topic/s, from one search window/box. Most libraries information provision is traditionally been centred on library catalogue. There is a view that all digital info-resources to be catalogued and made available that will be compatible to *Google's* or *Amazon's* search interface (western languages). This strategy in no time, will be found to be gigantic a task to handle, the amount of digital information is too huge and manually too costly an affair to cope with. But at the same time we must also remember that print material available in the library or borrowed, *vis-à-vis* the digital material obtained for the user, is accessible under contractual regulations. It would not be inappropriate to suggest for a library of national library type, to come to some agreement with *Google Scholar* with objective of making the NL's catalogues and all other bibliographic databases available through *Google Scholar*. This will increase the visibility of these resources to end users without shuttling from one to other search engine.

In terms of library as an organisation and its role as a concept, is of facilitating knowledge creation is sufficiently broad for individual library to develop services in new areas where they can probably add more value than trying to develop traditional role of information provision by continuously focusing on collection development on their own. Such a role would imply a closer integration with other socio-cultural organisations where the library would be perceived less as a monolithic institution and more as a part of network of services. In order to fulfil this role, it would be important for librariesto cooperate nationally and internationally in the area of information provision and to collaborate in developing the compatibility in new areas, such as, digital library services at the national level.

Earlier we have stressed upon the need of redefining "a librarian" in digital library context and emphasised creation of more points of entry into the profession. Over the last two decades the level of library professional education and training has been upgraded to bring out professionals with required knowledge of ICT application in library environment. Indian libraries and librarians involved in digitisation and handling with e-publications are fairly a competent lot as reflected in papers published in Indian LIS professional journals. Leaving aside a few exceptions, most of these are based on hand on experience of dealing with digital info sources, citation analysis, users' survey based on empirical data generated in house or from a selective group of libraries.

Our educational programmein librarianship has not kept pace with the needs of the scholarly community. The educational needs of librarians in order to be expert practitioners in their fields have changed many times and the rate of change is increasing fast. So far these schools are preparing both at entry level librarians and senior managers at the same time by following the same curriculum. Do we need all our library staff to study cataloguing and classification or learn how to handle several hundreds of reference sources?

Much of the work we do, particularly in academic and research libraries (including national library) in the digital resources environment where multimedia, multiple languages and multiple info-resources are to be dealt with simultaneously. These activities may have to be handled online in some situation. This would surelyrequire much more in-depth discipline specific knowledge than what we were having now. One of the most powerful uses of digital technology is to share scarce resources (e.g., *Dead Sea Scroll, India Office Records or South Asian Manuscripts Collections* in the British Library–*Google's* initiatives). Libraries have been digitising their special collections–individually, in joint operation, and as a group created to do specifically just that job. To handle such digital copies there is a need for in depth subject knowledge for collection development and generating metadata, and collection use at the same time.

In a large number of national libraries and many such well known university libraries of the world, LIS qualified professionals are mostly engaged in creating metadata, bibliographic and reference services. Parallel to this category of staff, we find language and subject specialists who are responsible for collection development in specially identified areas with curatorial assignments; another category of staff may be bracketed under experts with specialised training and background, in such field as, ICT, publishing, display and exhibition, preservation and conservation. The last two categories of staff do not required to have any LIS training or such professional degrees.

We believe our role is to be a catalyst – to allow scholarly communication process to move forward, to identify the linkages between academic disciplines and research libraries and both the traditional and digital information resources that support the growth of knowledge. Let us hope the newly constituted Working Group on LIS Education, constituted by the National Mission for Libraries (NML) shall suggest some proactive measures required to be adopted by all stakeholders to make the library profession in a new *avatar* to be sustainable.

References

1. Davenport, Nancy A.(2007): 'Digital Libraries And Librarians Of The 21st Century, in *Digital Information And Knowledge Management* ed. Sul H. Lee, NY, Haworth, 2007, 89-97.
2. Harsha Parekh (2004): *Digitisation In India; Developing And Implementing A National Policy*. ICDL, 2004, pp. 204-207.
3. Internet and Mobile Association of India (IMAI):http://www.imai/news/internet-subscribers-base-in-india-may-reach-150-mn-report/html (accessed 18/11/2012).
4. *Census Of India* 2011, V.I.http://en.wikipedia/wiki/2011_census_of_India.

5. Parkes, Dave and Waltoon, Geoff: *Web 2.0 And Libraries.* Oxford, Chandos, 2010, 13-29.
6. Parkes, Dave: *Ibid.* 56.
7. Jones,P.: –'Industry Divided Over Digitisation', *Bookseller,* 10th October, 2008. http://www.thebookseller.com/news/68795-industry-divided-over-digitisation-.html (accessed 16/05/2012.
8. Carlson, N.: http://www.businessinsider.com./2009/1/printing-the-nyt-cost-twice-as-much-sending-every-subscriber-a-free-kindle (accessed 17/09/2012).
9. *http://www.dailylit.com /books (accessed 10/11/2011).*
10. *http://www.scribd.comabout/ (accessed 10/11/2011).*
11. Mills, E.: 'Google ETA? Roughly About 300 Years Will Take To Index The World's Info,' *CNET News,* 8th October, 2005.
12. *Indian Express,* (20th December, 2012, editorial: 'Papyrus In Hi-res')
13. National Library of Scotland: *Breaking Through The Walls: The Strategy Of The National Library of Scotland,* 2006. http://www.nls.uk (accessed on 07/06/2012).
14. India – A Reference Annual, 2012; 239.
15. National Mission for Libraries (2012) <http://www.nationalmissionforlibraries> (accessed 07/09/12).
16. National Library, Kolkata Http://www.nationallibrary.gov.in (accessed on 11/07/11).
17. OCLC: http://oclc.org/reports/2003/pattern recognition/The 2003 Environmental Scan/Pattern Recognition Scan/ (accessed on 18/12/2012).

7
Transitional University Libraries

Background

In today's world, libraries are claimed to be intellectual foundation of a democratic society primarily by allowing free and open access to recorded knowledge. But now in the beginning of the 21st century the very survival of our libraries is seriously threatened. Fast growth of electronic media supported by similar research and development in information and communication technologies (ICT) are allowing every citizenry new vistas to access information, irrespective of its source or packaging format. Types of information a library traditionally provides, a substantial segment of that is now also accessible directly through INTERNET, to alargersection of the community. This is the noticeable trendsin a select number of university libraries in India and the western world. It is expected to be followed in more and more universities sooner than later. This trend is also being accepted as inevitable in several IITs and similar postgraduate academic institutions in India.

In contrast, a large majority ofuniversity libraries areusing computers for their house-keeping operations only due to economic and/or shortage of trained manpower available. There are libraries where card catalogues are used side by side with machine readable catalogues (for current materials) as retro-conversion is moving at a slower pace again for the reasons mentioned above. Many academic and research institutions that have introduced computers in several of their house keeping operations over the last two decades, including online catalogues, are finding lessernumber of readers using reading room spaceor visiting libraries; many are cutting subscriptions of print copies of journals and other library materials every year and many research oriented libraries are regularly procuring e-books as part of their acquisition programme. 'A large majority of our colleges (31,324) and universities (544) have introduced computer for several in house activities. Many are also subscribing *e*-journals, *Internet* access and a few having in house preservation programmes of special materials in digital format'[1].

Libraries in India in general (including academic institutions) are facing perpetual economic threats. However, the greater threat is the perception of technology will solve these problems and all that someone is to do is to search World Wide Web for any information one needs. We accept a vast amount of 'information' is indeed available on the *Web today* but it is not always coherent or up-to-date, neither it would be egalitarian. A section of our library authorities believe that the digital library will solve many of our inherent library problems. People fail to realise that these important experiments are not only time consuming but also very costly. Digitisation of library materials are not undertaken systematically in large scale under any unified national programme. Presently each institution is moving independently with its own meagre resources. Contrary to popular expectations, our current efforts are best characterised as experimental and uncoordinated. A section of senior bureaucrats, academics, librarians and technocrats are all seem to be waiting for the information revolution to arrive soon as they are hearing about it in the media. If we do not begin this digitisation our libraries, educational institutions and the very intellectual fibre of our larger society would inevitably slide downhill.

Cost Factors

1. ***Books, periodicals and other information resources:*** Librarians are facing a serious problem of preservation and

have been trying their best to draw attention of both policy-makers and academic community on the poor condition of bulk of pre-independence Indian publications in their stock. These print materials are brittle and fragiledue to high acid content of paper used and unfriendly extreme climatic conditions that prevail in this part of the world. A large section of these materials are becoming gradually unusable that contain the intellectual and cultural history of the nation of a crucial period. There area fewmore serious perennial problems faced by Indian libraries, e.g., crippling annual "book-budget" as compared to fast annual growth in book publications (including *e*-books) andfaulty book selection process together with the practice of receiving 'books on approval' from venders, which hasbeen introduced in Indian libraries by a few wholesale book trade giants. Over the last decade theannual budgetary grants of academic libraries may have increased considerably due to overall improvement in economic condition of the country. But the reality is a considerable number of academic librarieshave lost about 30 per cent of their buying power during the last one decade. If these trends continuetill 2020 the 'book grant' of our large academic and research libraries will have only 20 per cent of the buying power of what they were having 50 years earlier. This will indicatea 50 per cent loss of average in percentage terms, the buying power of university *libraries.*

1 : Delhi University, Central Library

Year	*Units*	*Cost Per Unit*	*Expenditure*
2007-08	2,831	1,321	37,41,866
2008-09	4,423	1,725	76,30,637
2009-10	4,668	1,513	70,64,163
2010-11	2,555	1,608	41,10,161
2011-12	3,172	1,375	43,63,401
2012-13	1,432	1,481	30,36,886

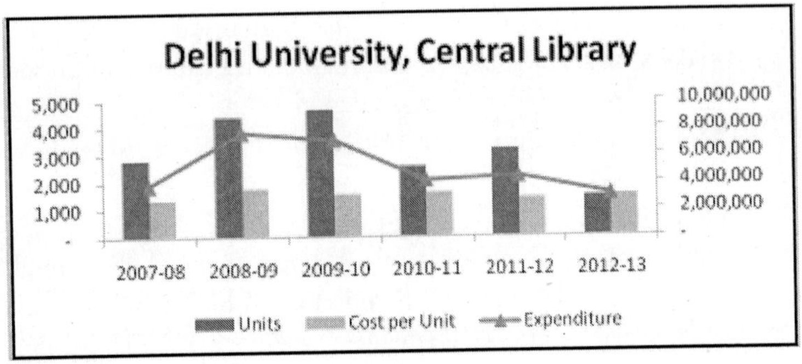

2 : Jawaharlal Nehru University, Library

Year	*Units*	*Cost/unit*	*Expenditure*
2005-06	3,615	1,080	39,06,516
2006-07	2,100	1,361	28,59,283
2007-08	7,309	1,670	1,22,00,000
2008-09	3,589	882	31,65,331
2009-10	223	2,447	5,45,860
2010-11	1,037	1,740	18,05,113
2011-12	2,207	3,333	73,58,137
2012-13	5,217	2,346	1,27,10,861
2012-13(eBooks)	1,813	4,412	80,00,701

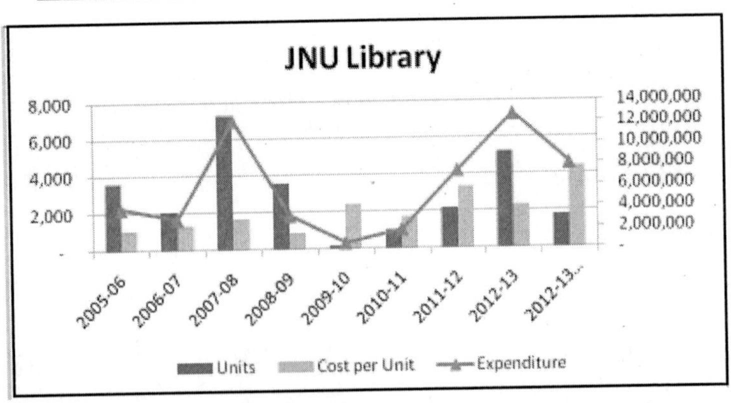

3 : H.E.M. North Gujarat University library, Patan

Year	*Units*	*Cost/unit*	*Expenditure*
2003-04	4,524	766	34,63,849
2004-05	3,575	645	23,08,979
2005-06	2,024	495	10,01,188
2006-07	2,323	597	13,87,709
2007-08	3,603	640	23,06,056
2008-09	3,274	46	1,50,046
2009-10	2,485	543	13,50,052
2010-11	3,512	693	24,34,310
2011-12	3,358	1,299	43,64,461
2012-13	1,537	1,255	19,29,290

North Gujarat University, PATAN

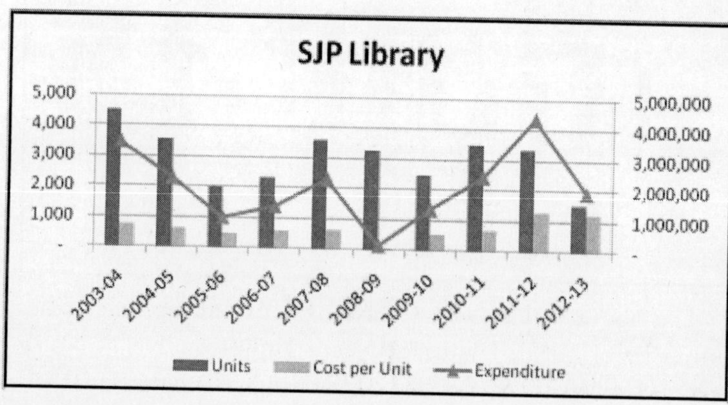

4 : IIT Delhi Library

Year	*Units*	*Cost/unit*	*Expenditure*
2003-04	1,846	2,186	40,34,638
2004-05	2,033	1,820	36,99,058
2005-06	1,483	3,141	46,57,493
2006-07	1,518	2,708	41,11,141
2007-08	2,364	3,162	74,74,489
2008-09	3,325	3,643	1,21,14,220
2009-10	3,252	3,377	1,09,81,938
2010-11	3,676	2,525	92,83,328
2011-12	1,253	3,395	42,54,441
2012-13	2,720	3,681	1,00,12,083

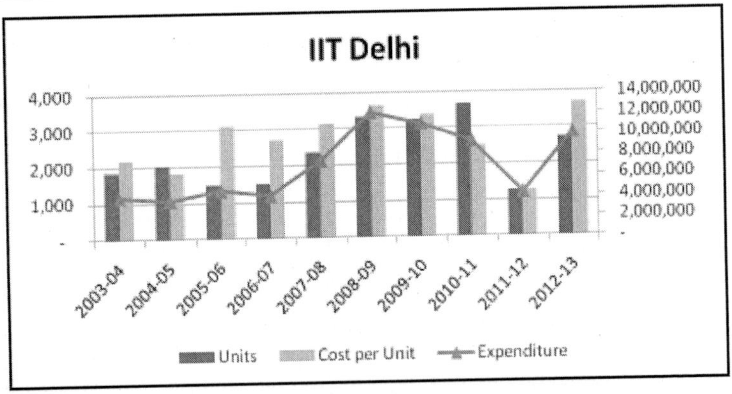

The above Tables and Charts of four Indian universities (University of Delhi, Jawaharlal Nehru University, Delhi, North Gujarat University, Patan and IIT Delhi) are reflecting their respective annual total number of books purchase for their respective central libraries, together with equivalent expenditure incurred. The figures for cost per unit (book) are obtained simply by dividing one by the other. We failed to tabulate required data earlier to FY 2007-08 of Delhi University as it used manual process for all book keeping records. These charts give ample evidence of continuous escalation in cost of publications over the previous decade. The relative increase in acquisition of books figure per year at North Gujarat University with smaller annual book budget is due to its policy of acquiring more Gujarati books (unit cost is less/book of local publications); whereas IIT Delhi acquires lesser number of titles every year while spending more than double under this head. A large majority of the items acquired by IIT Delhi are of overseas origin and on science and technological subjects which are relatively costlier than books on humanities or social sciences.

The problem is universal in nature worldwide. The problem has largely been partially taken care of, by a few prime research institutions as they were given adequate financial support and allowed to procure resource materials of their choice that helped in building up the largest, most complex and oldest collections of historical importance. These research institutions and academic centres have to assume a major social role in preserving and organising (creating partially) India oriented knowledge base that has been mostly, if not wholly, funded through public exchequer. In the USA, Europe, Japan, a segment of this is acquired through endowment funds exclusively meant for libraries/research organisations. It must be noted that majority oflndian main research centres are losing their library buying power and the main source of library funding is through government agencies (including state exchequers) that cannot perpetually meet this unending demands. Indian philanthropists are so few in number and that for library development exclusively, is too small a figure to be recorded here.

It is estimated from our previous research that average 40 per cent of printed resources in the field of STM (science, technology, management) annually acquired by these Indian research organisations are offoreign origin. Thus, the impact of inflationin price index and similar steep increase (10-15 per cent annually) in price of overseas publications (including journals) make a big dent in their respective annual budgetary allocations (especially with the current depreciative trends inthe value of Indian rupee, situation has aggravated further). Rapid increase in average price of library resource materials together with continued increase in the number of publications in different languages, worldwide, give us a clear indication of meagre stock Indian university libraries and other research institutions are acquiring is more and more a declining share of the world's output. Total number of titles published during 2010 is 2.2 millions according to *http://www.worldometers.info/books*[2]. Book publication figures of each country given hereare not of the same year for example, books published in the USA (2010): 328,259; UK (2005): 206,000; China (2010): 328,387 and for India (2004): 82,537 (Hindi: 21,370, Eng.: 18,752, rest in other languages)[2]. It is found through a random sample cheque (20 titles published in 2010) of seven online university library catalogues (1-Indian+3-USA, 2-UK and 1-Singapore), only about 17 per cent of the total annual average acquisition of book in science and technology fields were unique and the rest of the titles are copies of the same available in more than one library. One would naturally conclude that it would be impractical of continuing to build large costly warehouse type structures to shelve printed materials, thus replicating collections that exist elsewhere within the country.

The market for scholarly print and *e*-journals is in a state of upheaval and transition that has always been a perpetual nightmare for every academic library authority. Uncertainty of electronic journals is not restricted to scholars. Librarians are sceptical about their journal pricing models and licensing practices.

2. Personnel Cost: Whenever there is a debate on library funding, the focus tends to be on the acquisition of resource materials. But the other less apparent costs include the costs of cataloguers, reference librarians and other professionals are substantial, averaging about three to four times, if not more of the annual cost of acquisition in a typical university library of India. In most developed countries, there are several successful initiatives to develop cooperative and sharing arrangements to keep such support costs down. In India, we need to focus on this issue more vigorously as there is not much progress in sharing of HR talent or specialists within the Indian systems and services. It is a fact commonly accepted within the academic community that with the growth in volume of resources with diversity, scholarly helps increases the need for professional guidance in the use of such helps increases with it, e.g., language or non-print resources. Such professional guidance would come from subject bibliographers who are thoroughly trained to provide research support to scholars as well as to students at different stages of their academic pursuit.

'However, one must accept the reality of having proportionately lesser number of expert library professionals in future library systems irrespective of relatively increase in both volumes and patrons. One must also accept of having some increase in annual acquisition budget of academic libraries in general to partially offset the continuous inflationary trends in economy whereas the operational cost shall not see the same rate of growth; the ratios shall change significantly over the next decade. This trend is to be accepted as 'normal' considering the limited available resources (Hawkins, 1998)[3].

It is expected of having more and more information available in multiple formats. At the same time, library would be expected to provide more help finding, sorting and filtering the materials in different locations and sites. The gradual increase in number of users, the amount of information and the cost of hiring labour-intensive library professionals would make the current practice unfeasible. While in Indian context. we are yet unable to share or set up a panel of pool of experts on a national, local or at some specific macro-discipline scale. It is unthinkable to plan any significant increase in efficiency of personnel who would be available all the time to support the users' needs directly.

These facts and other relevant socio-technological forthcoming changes would ponder us to ask whether existing practice of collection development, which is already eroding, can be continued any longer. It would not be fair to expect any significant transformation soon in the way libraries support information needs of users by sorting, selecting and disseminating information because the crucial issue "filtering" will be greater due to rapid increase in volume of information sources. To find some satisfactory solution to this problem through some technological innovations is intriguing but a prudent library planner should expect increases–not decreases–in the human capital needed to help users to navigate through web network at least during the next few decades.

3. Storage Space Cost: We discussed the problems and cost of acquisition of new information sources but it brings in another set of costs of higher magnitudein the form of finding appropriate space for their storage and archiving the stock of information. Present practice of construction of new university library building is to provide storage space or stack area enough to accommodate print material for next 20 years. Such buildings are designed with the provision of expansion in the future. But the rate of growth of both print information sources and patrons or users in every academic campus have been moving faster than any of our previous perceptible limits, especially during the last two decades. This has resulted in overflow of information that are being retained in some make-shift manner or housed in some dormitory. To get adequate fund for an extension of the main library building constructed or to have a separate wing or even having a dormitory at an out of the way site is hard to come by especially in India where any such proposal may easily take ten years or more for implementation. The current cost of new library building is approximately @ Rs 2500 per square foot in an Indian metropolitan city. Hence, the cost of physically housing a single volume comes to about Rs 300. One has also to add to this the recurring annual expense of maintaining the building, cleaning of shelves, power supply, etc. Often these associated costs of housing and maintaining our library collectionsare ignored because space costs are not reflected in library annual budget estimates. The average cost of an Indian publication in English is Rs 600-700 (cost of an overseas English publication is more than double of this figure) and add to it the average inflation rate which itself shall exceed current Rs 300, the average maintenance cost/vol. within the next ten years. In contrast, the rapidly rising prices of books and other information resource materials together with continued annual increase in number of publications worldwide that are available for purchase, point us to the fact that academic and research libraries of India are surely acquiring annually a declining share of the world's intellectual output in print format.

Every university library of India is facing acute space problem in greater or lesser degree like their sister institutions all over the world. Compounded with this issue to the real life practice in library, particularly in an academic institution where about 10 per cent of the total collection is on heavy demand and the rest 90 per cent may be used/circulated infrequently. Of these again, there would be a vast majority shall never be used. By use or circulation of a book does not directly correlate with its value. By allowing access to information/knowledge recorded in the book/volume/document, by a library — no matter how often it is borrowed/consulted or referred to — strongly held value that considered as the fundamental mission of a library[4]. In the national perspective it would thus be considered as impractical to continue to build large, costly, warehouse type buildings to shelve printed materials largely duplicating collections that exist elsewhere.

*4. **Maintenance Costs:*** It has now been well established within the academic library world that the cost of electronic information storage is accepted to be relatively cheaper than the conventional preservation practices adopted so far by libraries. However, opinion differs on adopting digital technology for archival preservation of cultural heritage items, may not be the ideal reformatting process. Scholarly information in digital format would not only cheaper to deal with but also save avoidable duplication. Decaying of high acid content paper commonly used in India, must be treated, copied, or stored on some alternative format, if they are to be saved for the posterity. One must be aware of some unexpected challenges may arise with this new paradigm including, for example, the cost of updating the technology at regular intervals.

Future Strategy Faculty Support:

In the present economic context, pressure on higher education sector to mobilise funding more from outside sources than public exchequer shall gradually increase; increase in tuition fees and dramatic increases in library budgets shall be expected even at a slower rate. In India, a large percentage of higher education text books or books listed in curricula are being authored by faculty members. It is true most of the research activities in universities are being sponsored by government funding agencies in general. Whereas the faculty give away these intellectual property items produced by them, to some private organisations or to profit-making publishing houses that brings out as monographs and reports, etc. Most of the Indian higher education centres and universities do not have a commercially viablein-house publishing programme. In a few exceptional cases where the university has its own publishing unit, it is not run like other profit making commercial publishing house.

Part of the solution is to have academic institutions and professional bodies to become their own publishers and distributors of materials produced electronically, put on their respective web sites. The reality is university pays faculty to generate such scholarly writings that get published and distributed by some third party, retaining copyright in most cases; university acquires these publications for its library at a high cost again. In an electronic world, the university (or a consortium of research/academic institutions) retains the copyright, thus preserves the right of limited free distribution and address to overcome this large annual fiscal wastage. Universities should continue to support and encourage those institutions whose function is to make the results of research available on non-profit basis. This singular essential change in scholarly communication if accepted by the academic community would bring in a sustainable model for the research libraries of India.

We do not have any remedial national plan on this complex issue in place as yet. The National Mission for Libraries (NML) is expected to focus on sharing the cost of information resources and several other crucial issues and its deliberation followed by some concrete guidelines. However, as the years passed by, it is now so very uncertain to receive a formal report of this Committee containing some broad guidelines to be followed by Indian libraries and librarians, due to various uncertainties currently prevalent in the country. It is difficult for many of us to find out from the current literature,some 'thoughts orideas' expressed on the topic so far by an individual or a group within the profession. Sadly enough one of the members is being allowed to use NML web site to promote his private commercial venture. One must not hesitate to accept the reality that Indian academic libraries are passing through a state of stagnation in growth and direction over the last few decades by following the same accepted principles and guidelines of some western academic library systems practiced in mid-twentieth century. A large number of universities and research institutions have come up only during the last few decades. Libraries of these new institutions as expected, followed or replicated the same principles and policies adopted by the University Grants Commission (UGC) which were originally formulated under the aegis of Dr Ranganathan in early 60s. Whereas a large majority of university libraries of the USA and a few in Europe have taken appropriate moves in time, by accepting the writings on the wall; the library of the future will be less a place where information is kept than a portal through which students and faculty will access the vast information resources of the world. The most significant factor in this domain is the direct on going involvement of *Google, Amazon* and similar such commercial portals in a very big way to provide digital copies of all kinds of existing print materials, both current and old to any individual or organisation located in any part of the world. It is a known fact that in certain fields, more than half of documents/books are now produced and distributed only in electronic format. According to the present trends, primary formats for storing and delivering academic information resources shall more and more switch over to be in digital format; starting from materials in STM disciplines. Information resources in digital format are likely to continue to dominate as the medium of choicefor its universal accessibility *vis-à-vis* print media. Though using of such *e*-resources may get lesser weightage in several organisations, depending upon ergonomic and economic factors; the only other exception of preferring to go for a print copy, in Indian context, is of text books (school and under-graduate levels) or a recently published book for leisure or recreational reading. Evenprint item in these categories, would most likely be available within a few years, in digital format as well.

The prime responsibility of future library management and experts in India is to reorient management structure and work culture in our ailing libraries of higher education and research institutions. A solution to this problem (not so simplistic though) for libraries is to provide *electronic access to information* – rather than storage of information resources. The main advantage of having *e*-resources for a library and its users that assure of avoiding duplication of purchases that characterises the present system, were largely eliminated. This trend in access has been well accepted as the future model of access to information rather than purchasing a hard print copy byevery other library with the expectation of getting some user someday.

Over the last few years, we find several major academic and research libraries in India are consciously making efforts to digitise their respective special research collections that could be considered as part of India's socio-cultural heritage resources. These fragmentary actions by individual institutions are largely guided by their perceptions of preservation of both rare and 'heavily on demand' resources. At the same time, materials related to recent STM domain arenot being included for this purpose simply because of their short life-span and easy accessibility from other known electronic sources. The proposed *National Digital Library of India (NDLI)* would surely help to establish some standardisation for broad online accessibility, efficiency and affordability with minimum level of controlled plan of action. Ideally the *NDLI* is to act collectively to adopt some uniformity in reformatting technologies, to bring together all these digital heritage resources on their respective web sites to allow universal accessibility. This agency shall also hopefully, formulate a negotiated license grant policy for limited copying by libraries and individual scholars within the framework of Indian copyright legislation.The proposal is to establish a uniform national mechanism for collection of information in several formats, stored electronically in different locations, collected and shared via a centralised network agency. The old industrial age libraries (with card catalogue, rows of book shelves, indexing practices, etc.) shall gradually become more and more incapable of dealing adequately in this information age. But we must accept the fact technology alone cannot solve this problem. A commonly discussed solution to these problems is bysetting up an effective library/information resources centre that is competent enough to be technologically innovative to act as an electronic model where information access and delivery through the electronic distribution network–rather than handy storage of information resources physically–shall be the significant characteristics of a quality library of the future.

Distributing information over the network fundamentally changes the model library we all know and practice. There will be substantial reduction in cost (30 per cent) of electronic network distribution over the conventional print media (excluding the follow-up costs of handling, storage and preservation). Savings will be noticeable in paper, binding, mail distribution and printing and production processes. There will be cost intensive acceptable at the processing levelssuch as, editorial review, peer review, copy editing. However, some production procedures shall continue to be part of the game. It is believed that a closely related issue, like, copyright policy, shall get accordingly modified in phases, as we move forward more and more towards the electronic world.

A large majority of Indian academic institutions have realised that all types of information resources exclusively available in electronic format (in addition to digitally reformatted original print resources) shall take a long time to be a reality, if ever possible of achieving it. The cost of most of our university library services are borne by public exchequers where the end users are never being asked to pay per-view/use. The Annual gross tuition fees paid by the students in Indian academic institutions (including 'library fees', where applicable) is truly a drop in the ocean.In addition to all the stakeholders within the present system – author, publishers, distributers and end users – there is another major dominant stakeholder -Information and Communication Technologies (ICT), without whose full integration, access to electronic information resources is impossible. It is important to involve 'all stakeholders' in this process to allow the present practice of not charging the end usersor library patrons to pay-per-view to maintain the traditional values of our educational systems and the society at large.

What we have tried is to focus on the changing world of one of the major media of storage and preservation of our cultural heritage available in print format that have been in existence and an essential partner in the propagation of knowledge over last five hundred years, for the benefit of humanity. Earlier to that all our thoughts were being recorded, for example, stone inscriptions or manuscripts in variant formats. Today, we are facing the challenge of accepting another technological device that allows not only faster access to multiple sources of knowledge and information at different sites but also compound documents incorporating texts, photographs, videos and sound bites thus creating a multi-media environment to help in widening educational horizons. We all accept that the amount of information in our society is becoming overwhelming, and that we need to find more effective tools to find the information we require.

With the emergence of more libraries with larger amount of electronically accessible information, a whole new dimension of scholarship and educational programmes are to emerge. Texts and information stored electronically would allow a scholar or a layman with internet accessibility, to search a large amount of information, and to formulate new questions to find answers from wider varieties of resources. Thus, the 'extra information' may also incorporate documents in multiple media formats, such as, images, data tables, graphics, some creative art and archaeology including natural and other living objects, which would have direct impact on scholarship and learning process of the students at all levels. In IT field alone a large amount of technology and software have been developed to help the users to navigate through large amount of information but there is a considerable gap in the corresponding increase in number of computer accessibility in India that still remains a matter of concern.

'We realise that our current university educational pattern is not yet geared to the task of bringing out specialists with multi-disciplinary linkages. Whereas the electronic media supported by the fast growth of communication network is constantly pushing each individual to widen his or her perception of knowledge and its sources in a global perspective'[4]. University librarians of India are aware that the current practice of having a 'holistic campus library' cannot survivelong under pressure from the digital information world and users' accessibility through the global network environment. 'Bigger is better' is no more meaningful in an electronic age. We cannot afford this competitive approach as it will fail in terms of cost effectiveness, it would be ultimately destructive for the education system of the country. Pelikan[5] suggested, 'there is a dynamic relationship of research with teaching, and of both with the acquisition, preservation, and circulation of documents and artefacts, that applies to art galleries, museums, and above all to libraries'. We must come up with new models for the twenty first century, not try to sustain our old structures. The library of the future will be less of a place where information is kept than a portal through which students and faculty members will access the vast information resources of the world.

Relatively, older Indian university libraries (started before 1950s) followed the academic pattern more in line of British universities, of 'goingit alone' are already showing the signs of slowly breaking down. This is true both for the academic library and its parent organisation. It is largelythe economic factors that have been specifically ascribed to libraries in this chapter.

This reasoning would surely apply equally well, to academic institutions stressing the need for more inter-dependence with other similar institutions for sharing the resources and save the time of the readers. It is significant to notice that large number of research papers and dissertations that are being brought out from the Indian research institutions and universities since 2000, contain more and more reference citations from the web sites, irrespective of the subject it dealt. This indicates access to digital information is now a common phenomenon and secondly, technology allows researchers to look for information beyond their respective library collections by adopting Cloud computing devices. This new library needs to bring together scholars and information resources without necessarily bringing either one to a physical building having the conventional card catalogue and print copies of books.

'Cloud computing derives its name from cloud which represents data centres, technologies, infrastructure and services delivered through internet. However, with an upsurge in the usage of internet many organisations and educational institutions are either purchasing cloud based services offered by an agency, or building their own with required specifications based on one's own needs.

This new library needs to bring together scholars and information resources without necessarily bringing either one to a physical building. In a recent paper by Mayank[6] stated, 'adoption and implementation of any new technology like Cloud computing within an institution depends on technical factors along with the characteristics of the organisation that introduces the technology and the feedback obtained from the users'.

References

1. *India Reference Annual, 2012.*
2. http://www.worldometers.info/books (accessed: 10/04/14).
3. Brian L. Hawkins: 'Unsustainability Of The Traditional Library And The Threat To Higher Education, in Mirage Of Continuity, Hawkins and Battin ed., CLIR, Washington, DC. 1998. pp. 129-30.
4. *ibid.*, p. 136.
5. Jaroslav Pelikan (1992). *Idea Of The University: A Re-examination*, New Haven, Yale University Press, p. 113.
6. Yuvaraj Mayank (2013): Examining Librarians' Behavioural Intention to use Cloud Computing Applications, *Annals of Library And Information Studies*, Vol. 60, pp. 260-268.

8

Academic Research in Library and Information Science

Background

Teaching of librarianship in India at university level, started well before many European universities accepted this as a full-time academic programme. A few short term training programmes were being carried on by a few State level library associations before Dr Ranganathan started a one year fulltime course at the postgraduate level, in University of Madras in 1937 leading to B.Lib.Sc. He started conducting a similar course (1948-49) after he moved to Delhi to take charge of the University of Delhi Library. Only in the beginning (1948), it was conducted as B.Lib.Sc. From the next year, both the Masters and Ph.D. programmes were introduced. He acknowledged the need of introducing research and development as an integral part of the course curriculum. The first Ph.D. degree was awarded in this discipline in 1957 from the University of Delhi under his supervision. Over the years, nomenclature of the course has changed from 'librarianship', 'library science' to 'library and information studies/library and information science' at different universities. Since the days of its inception, the course curriculum, syllabi, teaching and training methods and formats have all been largely based on the diploma course conducted by the School of Librarianship and Archives, University College, London and regularly updated by the library schools as and when they felt the need of it. This process of 'modernisation' was naturally moving fast during the last two decades, due to the introduction of information and communication technologies (ICT) in various library applications. The senior professionals are finding it hard to keep pace with the technological changes that are being offered by vendors worldwide. There are now about 200 Indian universities, including a few open universities or centres of distance learning, providing full-time one/two year/s BLISc course; several of these are also offering one/two years MLISc course for students having a BLISc degree. In addition, several of these universities are also offering M.Phil. Ph.D programmes, mainly based on dissertation. We made an attempt to present the real life situation of LIS academic/ doctoral research activities essential for the development of librarianship relevant to a nation, region or an institution involved with library and information services and systems.

There is no coordinating agency and policy guidance to undertake LIS research outside the university domain. We do not have any organisational support as compared to research in scientific and technological fields, where government organisations like, Department of Scientific and Industrial Research (DSIR), Council of Scientific and Industrial Research (CSIR), Atomic Energy Commission (AEC), University Grants Commission (UGC) and several other public sector corporate bodies, provide funds and coordinate through a smooth and efficient infrastructure both for providing fund and to disseminate their research output. Indian Council for Social Science Research (ICSSR) provides similar funding support to social science research organisations and individual social scientists. Similarly, Indian Council for Historical Research (ICHR) supports historical research and Indian Council of Philosophical Research (ICPR) is responsible for funding research programmes on philosophy and religion. However, NASSDOC of ICSSR and NISCAIR of CSIR are active in providing grants in a limited way, for some bibliographic or documentation activities in their respective domain. A small part of their research grants are also offered to a few LIS postgraduate research students for their individual academic pursuits if the project topic could broadly be identified as part of Social Sciences or Science and Technologies. Research scholars in humanities or arts would be expected to receive grants for research in literature, performing arts and other creative activities, from the UGC or respective state or central academies. UGC has a provision of offering limited research grants to academic staff of higher education institutions in all disciplines, including LIS. In reality, a large majority of research scholars in India are expected to arrange their own funds, to pursue for M.Phil. or Ph.D. degrees in an Indian university. There is no specific public funding agency for research in LIS nor any private trusteeship or endowment fund available in support of LIS research in India till date. There is a proposal to create a public charitable trust to support R and D facilities in this field, from the savings of IFLA 1992 Conference to partly tide over this gap. This is perhaps the main reason why a large majority of researchers join the doctoral programme as a part-time student while holding a full-time job in some organisation, whereas, in other disciplines postgraduate research by and large are undertaken by full-time students/academic staff who are entitled to avail sabbatical leave for three years. There is nothing wrong for library staff to join the Ph.D. programme with the objective of keeping his/her options open in the job market for moving higher on the career ladder.

Before coming back to library and information science (LIS), we must discuss first the significant differentiations of the basic infrastructure of Indian R and D facilities in general, covering all significant disciplines. One may look at education-spending as a per cent of GDP and we find that India spends on education is respectable by international comparative standards, although a significant part of it comes from individuals and families, and not from governmental support. The gross enrolment at the higher education level (colleges and universities) in India is currently little over 18 per cent (China 22 per cent + is having the world's largest higher education system). The fact is that if we include all the colleges (post-secondary level), India has more than half the world's total higher education institutions which, in many ways is rather shocking and also indicates a certain lack of efficiency in the Indian system. A lot of these colleges, I think, are too small, even as teaching centres. The current salary structure in Indian academic institutions is considered reasonably well by international standard according to purchasing power parity.

India was following, by and large the British higher educational structure during the colonial period. But immediately after independence, a vast expansion programme of R and D activities was introduced under Jawaharlal Nehru, the first Prime Minister, more close on the existing Russian model, by setting up separate research centres in every major fields of Science and Technology primarily under the Council of Scientific and Industrial Research (CSIR). Gradually, several such research councils were established by the central government, for areas covering, social sciences, history and one for philosophy. Indian universities are mostly funded from public exchequer–mainly by the state governments and the University Grants Commission (UGC) set on the British model, as a body for disbursing grants to all the universities.

This new separate impetus for research and development bestowed upon a set of public funded institutions made the Indian universities more to act as academic degree (including postgraduate) level teaching centres. The only research, so to say, offered by an university for obtaining a Ph.D. degree, is always considered to be the preliminary level of any original research work, accomplished by a student (exceptional cases where D.Litt, D.Sc. are being offered). Thus, very little fund was made available to universities for research activities. This has resulted in some slackness and non-persuasive approach towards research after obtaining a Ph.D. degree by the academics, in general. This has also affected the universities by restricting their infrastructural growth, such as libraries and laboratories to a large extent. So far India has no national focus to improve its research programme of its universities despite the fact that several reports, including the National Knowledge Commission have recommended a variety of thoughtful suggestions and in a few cases, some are also being in the process of implementation.

Library and information science (LIS) has several components and peculiarities; activities close to a public service utility, and involved in the process of collection (information resources), storage, maintaining records of stock, analysis and dissemination of information, library management, maintenance and preservation of stock, etc. To undertake a research project in any of these fields, one has to consider the complexity and its multi-disciplinary nature would bring out some inherent difficulties in identifying an empirical research topic, followed by continuous changes induced within the system, due to changes in tools and techniques at different operational levels. According to P.S.G. Kumar[1] (1987) library schools attached to 28 Indian universities awarded 41 Ph.D. degrees and additional 31 degrees awarded on topics relevant to library science by other faculties of universities during 1957-1985. With the proliferation of library schools since 1980, there is a boom of Ph.D. degree holders in the LIS field. Since 2000, the annual output of our LIS schools is perhaps the highest both at the graduate and postgraduate levels (Ph.D. degree holders inclusive) compared to many other developed and developing countries of the world. We must take note of the fact that number of LIS schools at university level in both the USA and UK has been reduced as compared to what the figures were till 1990. INFLIBNET's database listed nearly 600 Ph.D. theses on LIS from 63 universities [listed 1,029 theses including several incomplete and duplicate entries]. Both Kumar and INFLIBNET stated categorically, the data on LIS doctoral degree are incomplete due to lack of 'full support' from the universities. We made an attempt here to present a quantitative analysis of data made available to us by INFLIBNET.

To this we incorporated (collated by Kumar) a few Ph.Ds that were not in INFLIBNET database.

Table - 1: Number of Ph.D. Theses Awarded by Indian Universities

S. No.	*University, Place*	*Language*	*Year/s*	*Total Ph.Ds*	*Remark*
1.	Agra University, Agra	H	1981	1	
2.	Aligarh Muslim University, Aligarh		2005,2006	2	*Corrupt INFLIB data
3.	Allahabad University, Allahabad		1966	1	[Not in IFLIBNET]
4.	Amaravati University, Amaravati		2007	3	
5.	Andhra Univ., Waltair		1982-2007	45	
6.	Annamalai University, Annamalai		1981 -2006	30	
7.	Benaras Hindu Univ., Varanasi		1984 -1998	16	
8.	Bangalore University, Bangaluru		1993 -2003	6	
9.	Berhampur Univ., Berhampur		1992, 1997	2	
10.	Bhagalpur Univ, Bhagalpur	E +H	1977-1978	4	1 Hindi + 3 Eng
11.	Bhavnagar Univ, Bhavnagar	E +H	1999, 2006	2	1 E +1 H
12.	BS Ambedkar Marathawada, Aurangabad	E + M	2003 -2007	7	2 in Marathi
13.	Burdwan Univ., Burdwan	E + Beng	1984 – 2008	21	4 in Bengali
14.	Calcutta Univ., Kolkata		1963, 1982-2007	5	[3 not in INFLIBNET]
15.	Calicut Univ., Calicut		1989 – 1995	4	
16.	Delhi Univ., Delhi		1957, 1977-2006	57	
17.	Gauhati Univ., Gwahati		1972 – 2004	6	

S. No.	*University, Place*	*Language*	*Year/s*	*Total Ph.Ds*	*Remark*
18.	Gulbarga Univ., Gulbarga		1975, 1983 - 2006	11	
19.	Guru Ghasidas Univ., Bilaspur	E +H	1998 – 2007	17	10 in Hindi
20.	Guru Nanak Dev Univ., Amritsar		1978, 1991 -2003	4	
21.	Harisingh Gaur Univ., Sagar		1992 – 2008	27	
22.	IG National Open Univ., Delhi		2007	1	[Personal contact]
23.	IIT, Delhi		1984	1	
24.	Jadavpur Univ.,Kolkata		1991	1	
25.	Jamia Milia Islamia, Delhi		1993	1	[Not in INFLIBNET]
26.	Jammu Univ., Jammu		1986,1999(2)	3	
27.	Jiwaji Univ., Gwalior	E + H	1984 -2007	31	7 in Hindi
28.	Kamraj Univ., Madurai		1985	1	
29.	Karnatak University, Dharwar		1981 – 2007	52	
30.	Kashmir Univ., Srinagar		2007	1	
31.	Kerala Univ, Thiruvananthapuram		1984, 1993-2003	4	
32.	Kurukshetra Univ., Kurukshetra		1992-2003	7	
33.	Kuvempu Univ., Shimoga		1997 – 2008	7	
34.	L.N. Mithila Univ., Darbhanga		1981- 1983	2	[Not in INFLIBNET]
35.	Lucknow Univ., Lucknow		2003 -2004	4	
36.	M.L.C.R. Patrakarita Univ. Bhopal		2006	1	

S. No.	*University, Place*	*Language*	*Year/s*	*Total Ph.Ds*	*Remark*
37.	M.S. University of Baroda, Vadodara		1972, 1983	2	
38.	Madras Univ., Chennai		2002 – 2008	11	
39.	Mangalore Univ., Mangalore		2002	1	
40.	Manipur Univ., Manipur		1989 – 2008	15	
41.	Mohanlal Sukhadia Univ.Udaipur		1997	1	
42.	Mysore Univ., Mysore		1984- 2002	5	[15 without
43.	Nagpur Univ., Nagpur		1980 – 2004	27	year]
44.	North Gujarat Univ., Patan	E + Guj	2002 -2006	10	[7 in Gujarati]
45.	North-Eastern Hill Univ.,Shillong		1995 – 2008	15	
46.	Osmania Univ., Hyderabad		1993 -2007	22	
47.	Pune Univ., Pune		1978 – 1999	8	
48.	Punjab University, Chandigarh		1977 – 2007	15	
49.	Punjabi University, Patiala		1992 – 2002	4	
50.	Rabindra Bharati Univ., Kolkata		1980	1	[Not in INFLIBNET]
51.	Rajasthan Univ., Jaipur		1980 – 2007	11	
52.	Ranchi University, Ranchi		1973	1	
53.	Ravishankar Shukla Univ.,Raipur	E + H	1977, 2002	2	[1 in Hindi]
54.	Sambalpur Univ., Sambalpur		1994 – 2007	8	
55.	SNDT Women's Univ., Mumbai		1997 – 2000	4	

S. No.	*University, Place*	*Language*	*Year/s*	*Total*	*Remark*
56.	Sri Krishnadevaraya Univ., Anantapur		1999 – 2007	3	
57.	Sri Padmavati Mahila Univ., Tirupathi		1997	2	
58.	SRT. Marathawada Univ., Nanded		1999 – 2007	3	
59.	Utkal Univ., Bhubaneswar		1991 – 2007	6	[D.Litt. – 1]
60.	V.M.Open Univ., Kota		2004 – 2005	4	
61.	Venkateshwar Univ., Tirupathi		1988 – 1995	6	
62.	Vidyasagar Univ., Midnapore		1996 – 2003	9	
63.	Vikram Univ., Ujjain	E + H	1992 – 2006	11	[1 in Hindi]
	Total :			595	[9 – Not in INFLIBNET]

There is a strong need of undertaking a bibliographic survey with critical analysis of research topics listed in INFLIBNET database. We notice both in the USA and UK majority of the doctoral degree holders are serving as faculty members. Unlike in India, a large number of them having equivalent academic qualifications are serving in some academic and special libraries. During the years 1950-1980, only one or two Ph.D. degrees were awarded by the LIS schools in a year. In the 1980s the rate has increased to double figure, on an average of 10-15 degrees were conferred annually. Since 1990s till date, the total annual output has increased at a faster rate resulting in such a large figure of 595 till 2008 (INFLIB database). This significant rise may be due to a big increase in number of LIS schools offering doctoral level research programmes during the last two decades. Although most of these dissertations were in English but some are available in a few other local languages (22 in Hindi; two in Marathi from B.S. Ambedkar Marathawada University; four in Bengali from Burdwan University and seven in Gujarati from North Gujarat University, Patan) [Chart – I]. According to the database, University of Delhi has awarded the largest number of doctoral degrees (57) followed by Karnatak University, Dharwar (52), Andhra University, Waltair (45), Annamalai University, Annamalai (30).

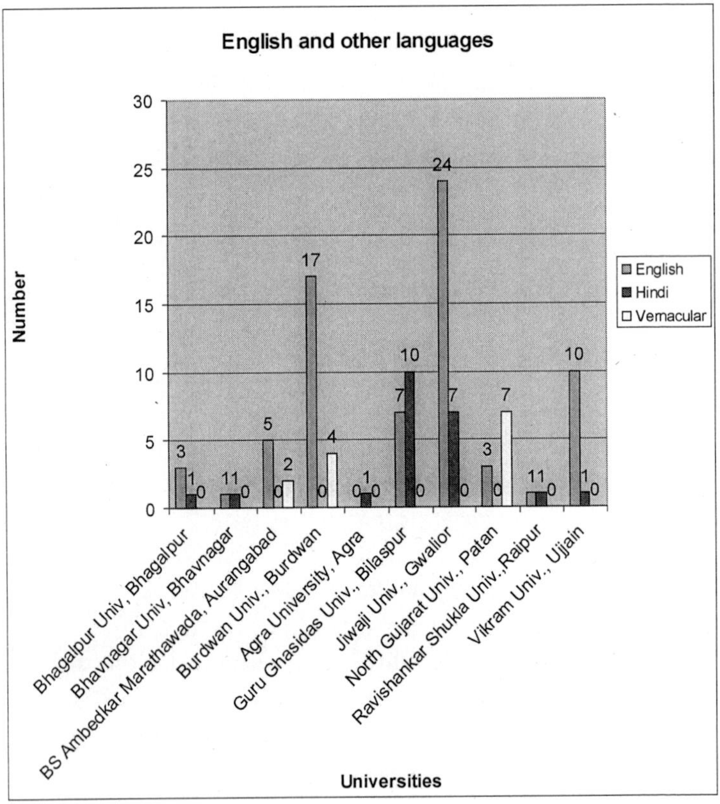

Fig.:1 – Theses submitted by candidates in different languages at universities

University of Allahabad is the first to award a doctoral degree in a topic of library science (*Library Movement in India*) in 1960 by the Department of History. The database provides the names of researcher but in several cases universities failed to provide the names of research guide. However, accepting this limitation, we find the following ten faculty members of different schools of LIS have guided the highest number of researchers with P.S.G. Kumar of Nagpur University claimed to be the toper (Chart: II). To the best of my knowledge, a former university librarian and head of LIS Department of North Gujarat University was having the distinction of supervising seven part-time research students simultaneously, who obtained Ph.D. degrees within five years, after getting registered with the university. It may not be an exceptional case in the present Indian context. Many of the senior LIS faculty members have guided research on any and every branch of library and information science irrespective of

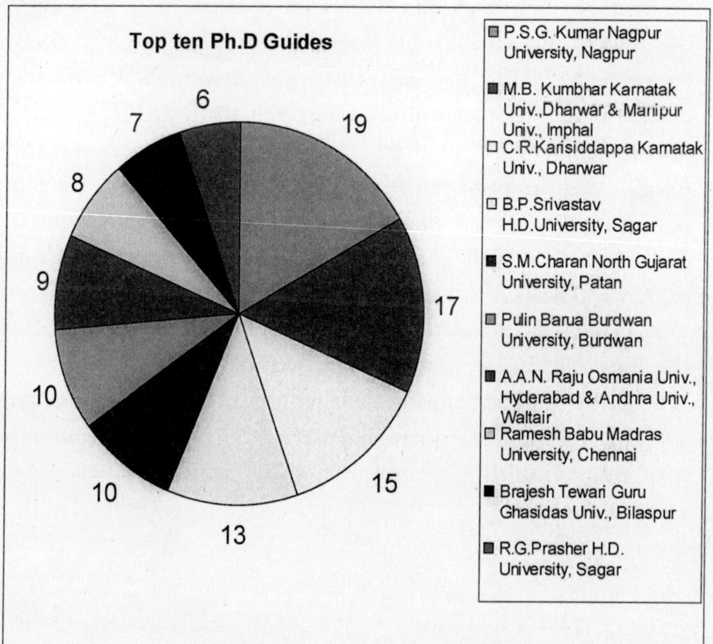

Fig : 2

their own specialised field/s. Current trend is to give preference to a doctorate degree holder for a faculty position in a library school. This could be the reason of having large increase of Ph.D. research scholars in LIS field.

Top Ten Research Guides

We attempted to present a broad outline of the topics of research undertaken by library science schools. Database did not help us much in this matter as most of the entries were under, library science, library and information science or some such terms as a broad subject/topic. To get some idea on the topics of research, we relied on the titles of dissertation as recorded in the database and those provided by Kumar (1987, p. xv). This also indicates the trends in selecting a topic of research and how it is changing with the passage of time (*See* Table 2). It needs to be highlighted that till date only 14 dissertations were undertaken in Indian universities on 'classification' and eight of these were awarded Ph.D. degree before 1985. Only six were completed during the last twenty five years. We must not overlook the fact that only one research work at Ph.D. level was undertaken on Ranganathan (*Influence Of Sanskrit Literature On Ranganthan)* in Burdwan University, 2007 in Bengali. We must not also fail to notice examples of research work undertaken and degree awarded on two contemporary library professionals, (1) *Critical study of works by P.N. Kaula*, (D.Litt., Utkal University, 1992) and (2) *Academic contributions in LIS by P.S.G. Kumar*, (Nagpur University, 2008); both were university librarians and LIS faculty members during their tenures of service. No qualitative analysis of Indian LIS doctoral dissertations can even be attempted with out consulting the original dissertations.

Table – 2: Distribution of Ph.D. Theses by Subject

Topic	*Number*	*Topic*	*Number*
Academic Library	14	Knowledge Management	1
Agriculture Library	15	Library and Information Service	16
Bibliographic Control	5	Library Cooperation	3
Bibliographic Database & Analysis	2	Library for Disabled	1
Bibliography-Persian Literature	1	Library History	12
Bibliometric analysis	52	Library Information Research	3
Biography	3	Library Legislation	4
Book Publishing	1	Library Management	34
Cataloguing	8	Library Network	10
Children's Literature- Hindi	1	Library Resource Preservation	1
Classification	14	Library Resources and Services	8
Collection Development	18	Library Science Education	10
College Library	13	Library Communication Process	2
Computer Application	19	Library Standards	1
Current Awareness Service	2	Manuscript Collection	4
Data Processing	3	Map Collection	1
Database Network	1	Medical Library	12
Digital Library	3	National Library–Bangladesh	1
Distance Education	2	Periodical Publications	10
Documentation Service	4	Personnel Management	28
Electronic Information Resources	5	Professional Association	1
Electronic Media Library	3	Public Library	28
Engineering College Library	3	Ranganathan, Dr. S.R.	1
Government Library	3	Reading Habits	3
Grey literature	1	Resource Sharing	5
Indexing	4	School Library	4
Industrial Library	4	Scientometric study	1
INFLIBNET	1	Special Library	16
Information and Communication Technology	12	Subject Index	10
Information Resources	4	Thesaurus Compilation	2
Information Resources-Newspapers	4	UNESCO, Role of	1
Information Retrieval Systems	16	University Library	47
Information Retrieval Systems Design	2	Users' Education	2
Internet Application	6	Users' Study	31

An exhaustive quantitative study was made of doctoral degrees, conferred (3,014 LIS dissertations) in the USA and Canada, from the inception of Graduate Library School at the University of Chicago (inception: 1926, first doctorate degree: 1930; school closed in 1994) together with the output of the remaining LIS schools till 2007 (Sugimoto and others, 2009)[2]. They worked from the MPACT[3] database which provides a comprehensive listing of 3,014 LIS dissertations conferred by 38 ALA-accredited schools in the United States and Canada between 1930 and 2007. This was downloaded from *ProQuest's Dissertations And Theses* database; keywords used: *Information Systems* or *Library Science*. This includes dissertation committee/ guide, title, and abstract information on the dissertation. Compared to their larger database with abstract, our data source (INFLIBNET) is full of so many shortcomings. By including abstracts of theses, the MPACT database allows users better searching advantage, e.g., actual topic and scope of the dissertation directly under each university. INFLIBNET claimed to have received data mostly online, in creating the database of Ph.D. theses (for LIS) covering the period 1980 to 2008 whereas Sugimoto's team got a complete record of theses data from 1930 to 2007. It is, however, possible that many universities may not have supplied a comprehensive and accurate list of dissertations. As a result, we find so many gaps and discrepancies in the database.

Research In LIS By Individuals

There is another section of research findings reflected in the form of journal articles and papers presented at professional conferences and seminars. This type of research activities are being continuously undertaken by professionals independently and/or by a small like-minded group of professionals, results of such activities are being regularly published as research papers, in different LIS professional journals. This universal human phenomenon or the urge of creativity in every inquisitive mind to find answers to why, where, how, when and who, are encouraging some of our library professional colleagues to pursue in research to reach a goal or find an answer to the question/s they are facing with. This is the most important sector of research in every branch of human knowledge that surely sustains its natural growth. India has been contributing substantially in the growth of knowledge in library and information science. However, it must also be noted this output both in qualitative and quantitative terms, are of late, having lesser impact. India is having, perhaps the largest number of LIS training schools in the world but HR strength in this profession is comparatively less than many other countries. In a recent analysis of abstracts of research papers listed in *LISA (Library and Information Science Abstract)* online version published by Cambridge Scientific Abstracts (CSA) using country name as key words (Patra and Prakash Chand 2009)[4], it was found that within the SAARC and ASEAN countries, India has brought out the largest number of research papers as compared to other countries in the two regions (India: 3,367; Pakistan: 418; Sri Lanka: 175; Bangladesh: 140; Nepal: 39; Bhutan: 19 and Maldives: 8; similarly, Singapore: 750; Malaysia: 566; Thailand: 248; Philippines: 248; Indonesia: 227; Vietnam: 163; Mayanmar: 41; Cambodia: 39; Laos: 25 and Brunai: 11 records.). 97.65 per cent of the papers from SAARC and 90.52 per cent of records of ASEAN countries are originally published in English language. However, we must accept the fact that *LISA* is not a comprehensive source database for records generated in these regions.

An issue that must be brought up in this context is the lack of a research agenda and a coordinating agency that would guide and focus on research essential for formulating library and information services and systems within the country. In general, researchers on library and information science are pursuing all research and survey activities in their own interest to find answer to problems faced in their day to day professional life. There is no such broad research area identified, by any such body or professional association, that of national importance to warrant special treatment by all. Results or research findings of such activities are expected to identify the causes of any shortcomings and provide guidelines for future course of action.

National Knowledge Commission (NKC)[5] in its booklet, *Libraries: Gateways To Knowledge*, 2007, Annexure-2 (NKC-WGL recommendations revised) expressed their concern on the extremely limited R and D activities in LIS field today. Much of the academic research works are confined to issues relevant to local situation and condition. Researchers commonly tend to select a research topic within the discipline or field they are familiar with or exposed to while pursuing for graduation andor post-graduation courses before or after joining LIS. The proposed institution (IILIS) would have two major functions: (a) to offer short term training programme in relevant sub-fields for LIS professionals and (b) to identify, sponsor and conduct R and D programmes in Library And Information Science. This recommendation, like many others resolved earlier is gathering dust for nearly ten years now.

To justify our concern, if we take the case of Great Britain as an example, the major source of research support within higher education sector are being provided by the eight (8) research councils. In addition, four funding councils are providing with extra direct funding only to universities. The Art and Humanities Research Council (AHRC)[6] support research and postgraduate study from traditional humanities subjects and all branches of arts. It included librarianship and information management. According to AHRC 2008 report the number and quality of application to the doctoral scheme within information science, journalism and librarianship is very disappointing. The most undersubscribed area was librarianship. Based on this 'Library, Archives and Information Management' sector of Museums, Libraries and Archives (MLA) is constituted to improve this situation. Another key influence on university funding was the Research Assessment Exercise (RAE) which conducted periodic assessments of the quality of research carried out at the higher education level in all the disciplines across the board. The Chartered Institute of Library and Information Professionals (CILIP)[7]: combined body of Library Association and Institute of Information Scientists) maintains a database of doctoral dissertations in British universities which can be accessed online [*not free*]. The list of publications of the British Library includes about two or three research reports annually related to various library issues of national importance. The purpose of bring out these facts on research in LIS fields in the UK is to make all the stakeholders in India alert of the ground realities with a hope the professional organisations and policy makers in India would take note of it and pursue appropriate actions.

It is not very encouraging to note or identify really scholarly and original research contribution brought out by Indian library professionals or faculty members. Dr Ranganathan made significant contributions in every sub-field of LIS. If we look at the present panorama, Ganesh Bhattacharya's POPSI technique of generating subject heading is an example, if not the only one till date. A good number of contributions are coming from outside India, particularly in the use and application of Ranganathan's facet analysis in the domain of Web searching and organisation. A few years back, a group of specialised professionals worked hard on *Indian Marc* but no follow up action for its implementation was undertaken by anyone or at any level.

For every discipline, 'research' is a major component to widen the horizon of knowledge. Unfortunately, we have been continuously neglecting this factor while reviewing library science education and training programme. This has indirectly influenced many of the policy decisions of larger library systems in India resulted in accepting ready-made application programme, hardware or practices developed by vendors for some libraries in developed countries and marketed with specification and standards suitable for their purpose. Surely, there are a few others in Indian library field whose contributions are also to be recognised that helped the profession to reach this height. It is true that India is having the largest number of LIS schools and faculty members attached to over 200 universities. Every year more than forty fresh Ph.D. degree holders are being attending university convocation ceremonies over the last few decades. Sadly the weightage bestowed on this amount of research work *vis-à-vis* the number of research papers published annually, including their citation statistics, are rather insignificant.

There is an urgent need for further study of the relationship between the health of the doctoral programme and health and ranking of LIS schools. Another issue for consideration is the strength and weaknesses of the schools that have been bringing out highest doctoral degree output. The bottom line is we do not have any research in library and information science field at institutional level, other than the doctoral programme. Professional bodies have not take up this issue at any national forum neither they are generating the kind of resources required to support research activities. The National Library or libraries of national importance, receiving grants from central government, have not been sponsoring scholarly or professional research projects other than bringing out historical monographs or printed volumes of specialised catalogues—an issue that must be prioritised in all appropriate LIS forums. Lack of any serious research agenda in library science is the root cause of stagnation, we all are facing over the last few decades (post-Ranganathan syndrome!). We all know funds for projects are provided by government agencies and other public sectors (e.g., MIPP; The Mahabharata Database, Bibliography of Hindi printed books, Translated works in Hindi, and many more by Central Secretariat Library, Ministry of Culture). We need to identify an organisation, such as RRRLF or some such body (proposed National Commission for Libraries) is to have a large allocation of funds for sponsoring research (outside the academic domain) that would be available to allow any serious research activity of national importance to further professional growth.

We have the latest policy document, *Libraries: Gateways To Knowledge* (2007) on the future of LIS in India from the National Knowledge Commission (NKC) which set up a Working Group on Libraries (WGL). The group took into account the views of a section of senior professionals in formulating the recommendations. But neither the views expressed by the professionals nor the WGL have justified these recommendations based on any empirical data, literature search or a national survey involving all the stakeholders. In other words, no research work was undertaken in presenting such an important policy document. Same is the fate of follow up status in most of the reports submitted by the committees and commissions relevant to our library world. On the other hand, let us stop for a while and spend some time to do some reading of relevant literature on the topic now available both in hard and soft copy formats. In the UK[8], most of the major policy decisions were formulated after some fact finding research/survey, analysis conducted by a group of experts/group specialised in or professionally competent in undertaking such activities. Similar is the story in the USA. For all these research activities, funds are being provided by an appropriate trust or government agency.

References

1. Kumar, (P. S. G.): *Research In Library And Information Science In India*, Delhi, Concept, 1987.
2. Sugimoto, (Cassidy R.), Russell (Terrell G.) and Grant (Sheryl): 'Library And information science doctoral education' *J. of Education and Information Science*, 50 (3), 2009.
3. MPACT database: http://www.ils.unc.edu/mpact/dissertations/(accessed 25/02/10).

4. Patra (Swapan K.) and Prakash Chand. Library and Information Science Research in SAARC and ASEAN countries as reflected through LISA. In *Annals Of Library And Information Studies*, 56(1), March 2009, pp. 41-51.
5. National Knowledge Commission: *Libraries, Gateways to Knowledge: A roadmap For Revitalisation* (based on the Recommendations of the Working Group on Libraries), 2007.
6. Art and Humanities Research Council, UK.
7. CILIP Policy For Information And Library Research, 2005: http://www.cilip.org.uk/professionalguidance/research/researchstrategy.htm (accessed 02/03/10).
8. Nicholas (David): 'Research' in *British Librarianship And Information Work, 2006, 1-2005*, ed. by J.H. Bowman, Aldershot: Ashgate, 2007, 361-371.

Index

A

Advisory Committee for
  Libraries(HRD Ministry)
    terms /conditions for libraries, 87

Amazon, 102, 109

Analysis of
    Value Added
    by British Library
    -Arrow & Solow, 40

Audio Visual Material, 73

Autonomy, 31

Average cost
    of EHSU books, 56

B

Bhasa Bhavan
    Opening (2004), 35
    Building Design, 35

Bibliographic Control, 75-76
    Centralisation, 75-76

Bibliographic data access, 54

Bibliographic Division, 21

Book Publishing - India
    trends, 50
    rank, 50
    growth trend, 50-51

Books
    Grants/Budgets, 115

British Experience, 39

British House of
    Commons, Culture,
    Media and Sports
    Select Committee
    Report, 91

British Museum Library
    (Calcutta) author
    employment in, 10

Building Costs, 122

C

Calcutta University Library
    author employment in, 10

Cataloguing and Classification
  process- wastages, 75

Central Govt. initiatives origin, 86

Central Reference Library(CRL) –
  Kolkata, 22
    and National Library
      Unification, 43-44
    shifting to Delhi, 43, 65
    seperate identity question, 59
    merger, 11

Central Repository Library Systems,
  21

Central Secretariat
    /NASSDOC Libraries
    takeover proposals, 65

Central Secretariat Library(CSL)
    New Delhi, 36

crisis/staff crunch, 36
merger suggestions, 36
Cloud Computing devices, 131
Computer Application
/Manpower Training, 77
Computer/ Communication
Technology
introduction, 14
Copyright Act - 1957, 13, 63
Copyright Act - UK, 63
Copyright Act -US, 63
Cost factors
Books Publications, 115
CRL, 22

D

Delhi University Central Library
Books Expenditure-2007-2013, 115
Delivery of Books Act
-1954, 11, 20 ,44
Revised, 58
impediments, 64
Revision, 76
Limitations
/ineffectiveness,48
amendments, 51
obligations, 52-53
Penalty/default, 52-53
Delivery of Publications
(National Library) Act, 58
DELNET, 81
Digital Copies, 55
Digital Information Resource
issues, 95
factors, 96
concerns, 97
Digital Library role, 108
Digital Technology uses, 110
Digitisation
purpose, 102
efforts, 127
limitations of, 114
cost factors, 114
Digitisation of Library Based information, 15
Directory of Indian *Libraries*
online database, 70
DK Book Service supply pattern, 76

E

e - Resources
- advantages, 126
Early experiences (author), 9
Eastern Regional Library
Development Programme,20
E-Books, 98-100
e-format, 55
EHSU languages, 53, 55
books costs, 56
Electronic Media growth, 113
Electronic Media/ICT
impact of, 80
Extension Services, 73

F

Facebook/Twitter, 99
Faculty Members
as Authors , 124
and In-house Publishing issue, 124
Federation of Indian Publishers, 22
Fund Allocation/Expenditure, 74

G

Gandhi Rajiv
 at National Library -Kolkata, 35
GOI Dept of Culture tenure-author, 10
Google Books, 101, 109
Google/Amazon, 126
 role, 15-16
Grants
 utilisation of, 40
Guidelines for Legal Deposit Legislation, 47

I

ICT, 105
 growth, 16, 113
 role, 45
 in libraries, 53
 availability, 77
IIT Library
 Books Expenditure
 -2003-2013, 118
Independence
 Public Libraries during, 83
Indian DB
 (Public Library) Act, 64
Indian Language Books
 in National Library, 54
Indian National
 Bibliography(INB), 21, 57-58
 Catalogue downloads, 44
India's Legal Deposit
 legislation, 13
INFLIBNET
 support, 45
Internet Scenario
 - India, 98
ISBN Centre, 23
ISBN/ISSN, 22-23
 allocation/responsibility, 22

J

Jawaharlal Nehru Bhavan
 Site, 43
JNU Library
 Books Expenditure
 -2005-2013, 116

L

Legal Deposit Act
 system, 54
 role, 48-49
 issues, 49
Legal deposit System
 UK, 54
Librarian
 redefining role after digitisation, 109
Librarianship
 education, 110
 segments, 39
Libraries ICT use in, 113
Library role/ concept, 108-109
Library Acts, 21
Library and Information
 Science(LIS)
 education& training, 78
 Universities, 78
 Components, 137
 Future in India, 151

Schools, 137
teaching/doctrates, 17
Research limitations, 134
funding, 134
nature, 146
agenda, 147-48
support, 148
Library bypass, 106-107
Library mergers
proposal, 65
Library Schools, 44
Library Services
components, 71
limitations, 72
Library spending
government grants, 54
Library Staff, 29-30
Upgradation, 30
LISA(Library and Information Science Abstracts), 17

M

Maintanence Costs, 123
Manmohan Singh
at National Library -Kolkata, 35
Manpower Selection, 31
Measuring Our Values
- Arrow and Solow, 40-41
Mirage of Continuity
-B.L Hawkins, 15
Mobile Phones Schemes
for reading Books, 101
Modernization Programme
Libraries, 55

N

National Commission
on Libraries(NCL)
proposal for, 89
need, 89
National Conference on
the National Library
(NACONAL)-2006, 34
initiatives, 37
National Digital Library
of India(NDLI), 45,104, 127
objective, 45, 103
National Educational
Resource Centre(NERC)
- HRD Ministry, 22
National Knowledge
Commission(NKC)
Recommendations, 34
Role and Strategy, 38
WGL(Working Group
of Libraries), 34
..formation, 35
National Library - Kolkata , 8,19
Functions,19
Guidelines/initiatives, 20
objectives, 20
Reading Room, 23
Bhasha Bhavan Bldg, 23-24
measures taken, 105
Digitisation, 96
..project, 104
annual books received, 56
combined collection, 65

Exhibition, Display, Promotion and Publicity, 28
vacant posts,35-37
News Letter, 27
Building Underground Linkage, 25
Scholars Hostel, 26
Publication/Research Programme, 26-27
National Library Act
-1976
Action Plan/Proposals, 41, 58
National Mission
for Libraries(NML), 37, 42, 89
on sharing Costs of information resources, 125
Resolution, 104,
National Policy for Library and Information System- 1986, 13
National Social Science Documentation Centre (ICSSR), 36
and CSL, 36
NKC-WGL
(Working Group of Libraries), 34
Formation, 35
North Gujarat Univ
- Patan
Books Expenditure
-2003-2013, 117

O

Online Database, 15-16
Online National Bibliography(INB), 44
Outsourcing, 108

P

Paperless trends, 100
Parekh Harsha
on Concerns of Digitisation, 97
Pattern Recognition Scan
- OCLC, 107
Perception of
LIS-OCLC Report, 91
Performance Evaluation Critria(PEC), 87
Personnel Cost, 120
Ph.D Degree in LIS, 136-37
Awarded by Indian Univs, 138-41
Subject-wise, 145
Ph.d Guides
in LIS
..Top ten List, 143-44
Press and Registration of Books Act - 1867, 13, 60
amendments/practice, 60-62
Public Library
numbers in India, 70
aspect, 64
in DB Act, 64
term/concept, 69
Development concept, 91

Publication Bodies, 76
Publications
definition (DB Act), 58

Q

Quality of Books, 73

R

Ranganathan Dr S.R., 16
Raja Rammohun Roy
Library Foundation
(RRRLF), 70-71
Organisation set up, 84
functioning, 84
schemes, 84-85
grants 2011-12, 85
proposals for, 74
Annual Report 201-12, 83
Online Database Project, 87
Publications, 88
Ranganathan, D.,
PG Programme
- Madras-1937, 133
Contribution, 149
Readers Guide to
the National Library, 27
Reading Material, 72
Research & Development
facilities- India, 135
impetus, 136
Research Support
in LIS, 148

S

SAARC/ ASEAN
Countries
and LIS Research, 147
Satish Chandra Prof, 39
Committee Report, 39
Saving through Digitisation, 128
Seminars and Conferences, 29
Sinha Committee Report
Recommendations, 88
-followups, 86
Social Science Research
funding, 134
South Asia Accession List, 76
Storage Space
Costs, 122
Suggestions
for Libraries, 12

T

Technology Modernisation, 80
Touch Screen Devices, 100
Training Programmes, 133

U

UK Library System, 21
UNESCO Public Library
Manifesto-1994
on Public Libraries, 71
Universities
teaching Library Sciences
- India, 134, 137
Courses offered, 134

University Libraries
- guidelines followed, 125
University Publishing Unit, 124
UPSC/SSC
role, 31, 43
US Library of Congress
-Washington
Buildings, 25
experience, 39

W

Web 2.0, 99
Wikipedia, 99
World Libraries
responsibility, 21